WHO ARE THESE PEOPLE Anyway?™

The
BUSHES

Reuters NewMedia Inc/CORBIS

THE BUSHES

This publication is not sponsored or endorsed by, or otherwise affiliated with, any of the persons mentioned within. Any opinions expressed are solely those of the authors.

Photo Credits: clockwise from right: Owen Franken/CORBIS (Barbara Bush), Reuters NewMedia Inc./CORBIS (George P. Bush), Reuters NewMedia Inc./CORBIS (George W. Bush), Reuters NewMedia Inc./CORBIS (Jenna Bush) and AFP/CORBIS (Jeb Bush); back cover – Reuters NewMedia Inc./CORBIS (George Bush).

EDITORIAL

Managing Editor:	Jeff Mahony
Associate Editors:	Melissa A. Bennett
	Gia C. Manalio
	Mike Micciulla
	Paula Stuckart
Assistant Editors:	Heather N. Carreiro
	Jennifer Renk
	Joan C. Wheal
Editorial Assistants:	Timothy R. Affleck
	Beth Hackett
	Christina M. Sette
	Steven Shinkaruk

WEB

Web Graphic Designer:	Ryan Falis

PRODUCTION

Production Manager:	Scott Sierakowski

ART

Creative Director:	Joe T. Nguyen
Assistant Art Director:	Lance Doyle
Senior Graphic Designers:	Marla B. Gladstone
	Susannah C. Judd
	David S. Maloney
	Carole Mattia-Slater
	David Ten Eyck
Graphic Designers:	Jennifer J. Bennett
	Sean-Ryan Dudley
	Kimberly Eastman
	Melani Gonzalez
	Jim MacLeod
	Jeremy Maendel
	Chery-Ann Poudrier

R&D

Product Development Manager:	Paul Rasid

ISBN 1-58598-086-2

306 Industrial Park Road
Middletown, CT 06457
www.CheckerBee.com

Table Of Contents

Who Are These People Anyway?™

W ho are these people anyway? They're our new president, George W. Bush, and the members of his family, of course. Who are they, really, and what are they like? It's a natural curiosity to wonder what this man and his family are about, since he'll be running our country for at least the next four years.

Inside, you'll find fascinating profiles for our 43rd president and his immediate family, including his siblings, nieces and nephews, parents, grandparents and great-grandparents. How did each family member get started in politics? How did they meet their spouses? How do they feel about living the life of a Washington insider? You'll find the answers to these questions and so much more!

In addition to the inside scoop on the Bushes, you'll also learn how the Bush political dynasty originated and find out how the Bushes like to spend their time. You'll even do some time travel – taking a look back at the historic election of 2000 and then taking a light-hearted look forward at what we might expect to come from the White House in the next four years. There's so much fun information packed inside, you'll surprise your friends with all the great stuff you know!

George W. and Laura watch the fireworks celebrating the end of the 2000 presidential campaign.

The Who Are These People Anyway?™ series brings today's celebrities right into your living room. Other books in the series spotlight movie and television stars, talk show hosts, sports superstars and more! Check out our web site at **www.CheckerBee.com** for more details about the series that really sizzles!

The Bush Dynasty

Like the great dynasties of times past, the modern-day Bush political dynasty has been built on principles of hard work, determination and public service. Their philosophies are easy to understand, but how they were able to make it all happen is less well known.

The Dynasty Begins

It all started when Prescott Bush, the son of the well-to-do president of a Columbus, Ohio–based steel corporation, married Dorothy Walker in 1921. Dorothy's family was wealthy also, and she was educated at the best private schools money could buy. Their union was pivotal, as it merged two very influential American families and was the starting point for what would become the Bush dynasty.

Dorothy and Prescott settled in Greenwich, Connecticut, and Prescott worked on Manhattan's Wall Street as a financier. He was active in politics in his community, but soon longed for a bigger slice of the political pie. He ran for the U.S. Senate in 1950 and was defeated – but only in regard to the ballot, as his spirits remained strong. He ran again and was voted in, and ran successfully four more times after that. He resigned after 10 years, citing health concerns.

George Bush Presidential Library

In the meantime, Dorothy stayed home and raised the Bush brood – Prescott Jr., George, Nancy, John and William – concentrating on etiquette, religious teachings, strong will and determination. Because the Bushes had a fair amount of wealth, the children received excellent educations and all of the best opportunities.

Prescott Bush was involved in local politics and became a U.S. senator from Connecticut. He is pictured with his wife, Dorothy Walker Bush.

The Dynasty Expands

Prescott's son George was the next to carry on the family's legacy of politics – and of marrying well. After completing a tour as a Navy fighter pilot in World War II, George married Barbara Pierce.

George Bush Presidential Library

Barbara's family lived in Rye, New York, just over the border from Greenwich. Her father was the president of the McCall Corporation, owner of McCall's magazine. Barbara's lineage is as impressive as her husband's – she's a descendant of 14th president of the United States, Franklin Pierce.

After graduating from Yale, just as his father had, George and his family headed to Texas. There George hoped to find his fortune in the oil industry. Fortunately, his

George and Barbara with their four sons (l-r)
George W., Jeb, Neil and baby Marvin.

father had made alliances within several major oil corporations in the United States, and these relationships were helpful to George's success in this area.

George soon began to set his sights on a life in politics. He got his first taste of Washington, D.C., when he worked on Dwight D. Eisenhower's presidential campaign in 1952, which was also the time that Prescott was making his second run for the U.S. Senate. It would be more than 10 years later, though, after his father stepped down from the Senate, that George would look toward Washington, D.C. again.

Like his father, George lost his first Senate bid. However, in 1966,

Blue-Blooded Bushes

Did you know that George W. is fourteenth cousins with Queen Elizabeth II, the current queen of England?

two years later, he was successful and picked up his family (which by now had grown to include George W., Neil, Jeb, Marvin and Dorothy) and moved east. He served two terms that were, by most accounts, successful.

George Bush Presidential Library

George, Barbara and Millie enjoy their getaway by the sea.

A series of political appointments were next in George's career. He was named Ambassador to the United Nations, head of the Republican National Committee and U.S. Envoy to China. The biggest appointment in George's political resume came in 1976, however, when President Gerald Ford named him director of the Central Intelligence Agency.

In 1980, George made a run for the biggest post of them all – president of the United States. Unfortunately, his party nominated Ronald Reagan instead. However, Reagan soon tapped George for the vice presidency and the pair went on to control the White House for 8 years. When Reagan reached his term limit, George ran for president in 1988 and was elected easily.

The Dynasty Endures

Since losing a presidential re-election bid in 1992, George has stepped back from being the leading political voice of his family and has let his children pick up where he left off. Two of his sons have made their own political forays and have reached similar degrees of success as their father and grandfather before them.

Jeb Bush, George's second-oldest son, is serving his first term as governor of Florida. He and his wife, Columba, are actively working

Happy 75th Birthday, George! In March of 1999, the entire family came together to celebrate. (Front l-r) Neil, George W., George, Jeb, Marvin, Dorothy, (Back l-r) Sharon, Laura, Barbara, Columba, Margaret and Bobby.

to aid the poor, increase educational standards and create an appreciation for cultural diversity within the state.

And then there's George W. Bush, former oil tycoon and governor of Texas, who's now the 43rd president of the United States. George W. and his father are the second father-son team to make it to the Oval Office. The other pair are John Adams and his son, John Quincy Adams. At that time, the public deemed the younger John Adams "Q," in order to differentiate him from his father. It looks like today's American public will be doing the same, as George W. Bush has been tagged with the nickname "W."

Now growing in size and stature, the Bush empire can only increase in influence. Many political analysts have speculated that after George W.'s term in office, his brother Jeb may make a beeline to 1600 Pennsylvania Avenue. And if not, there's always George P. – George Prescott Bush. He's Jeb's son and he has already made a positive impact on the American public in his campaign efforts on behalf of George W.

The future is unclear, and predictions are impossible to make. But if the past is any indication, we can expect to see many more Bushes in public office through this century and beyond.

The BUSH *Family*

Samuel Bush
Great-Grandfather
1863-1948

Flora Bush
Great-Grandmother
1872-1920

Prescott Bush
Grandfather
1895-1972

Dorothy Bush
Grandmother
1901-1992

The George Bush Family

George Bush
41st President
Born 1924

Barbara Bush
Former First Lady
Born 1925

George W. Bush
43rd President
Born 1946

John Ellis "Jeb" Bush
Son
Born 1953

Marvin Bush
Son
Born 1956

Robin Bush
Daughter
1949-1953

Neil Bush
Son
Born 1955

Dorothy Bush Koch
Daughter
Born 1959

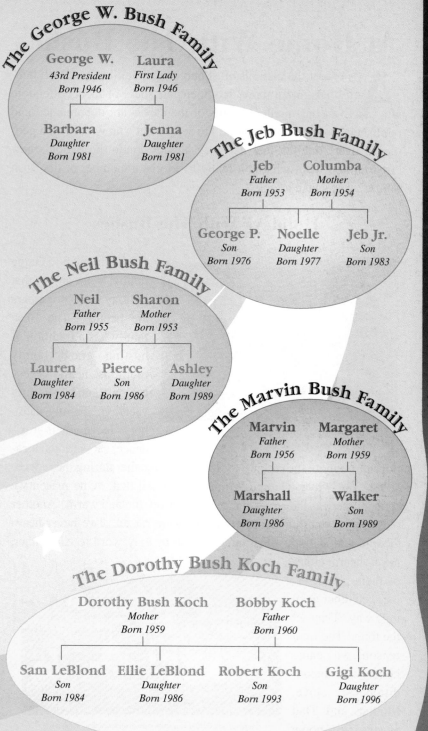

The George W. Bush Family

George W.
43rd President
Born 1946

Laura
First Lady
Born 1946

Barbara
Daughter
Born 1981

Jenna
Daughter
Born 1981

The Jeb Bush Family

Jeb
Father
Born 1953

Columba
Mother
Born 1954

George P.
Son
Born 1976

Noelle
Daughter
Born 1977

Jeb Jr.
Son
Born 1983

The Neil Bush Family

Neil
Father
Born 1955

Sharon
Mother
Born 1953

Lauren
Daughter
Born 1984

Pierce
Son
Born 1986

Ashley
Daughter
Born 1989

The Marvin Bush Family

Marvin
Father
Born 1956

Margaret
Mother
Born 1959

Marshall
Daughter
Born 1986

Walker
Son
Born 1989

The Dorothy Bush Koch Family

Dorothy Bush Koch
Mother
Born 1959

Bobby Koch
Father
Born 1960

Sam LeBlond
Son
Born 1984

Ellie LeBlond
Daughter
Born 1986

Robert Koch
Son
Born 1993

Gigi Koch
Daughter
Born 1996

At Home With The Bushes

As one of the nation's most publicized families, the Bush family has gotten more than their fair share of media attention. Even the smallest details of their lives are documented and published across the nation for all to see. So, it's no wonder that people all over America feel like they already know the nation's new "first family." But what is it really like to be a member of the Bush family? Let's take a look.

Holidays With The Bushes

The Bush family gathers around the kitchen to watch George make Tamales in Kennebunkport, Maine, during the summer of 1988.

With such a large family, you can bet that holiday get-togethers are hectic! The Bush family has a tradition of hosting grand family reunions nearly every holiday and summer vacation. Family members leave their residences at various locations throughout the country to flock to be together during these occasions. But why? George W. once explained that, "One reason we came home was the atmosphere was comfortable and warm. Another reason we came home is the way we were raised. I've never heard George and Barbara Bush utter a harsh or ugly word to each other, never heard either of them characterize each other in an ugly way. They set the tone. The final reason we came home was unconditional love. Mother and Dad always had a home

George and Barbara sit amid their ever-expanding family at their picturesque home, Walker's Point, in Kennebunkport, Maine.

of love. They loved each other and there was no question they loved us children." With an atmosphere like that, who could stay away!

Fun In The Sun

Another Christmas holiday tradition is to head to Florida for a quick vacation between Christmas and New Year's Day. The Bushes have gotten together in Boca Grande on tiny Gasparilla Island (found off the Gulf Coast near Fort Myers) on several post-Christmas visits over the past decade. The year 2000 was no exception, as the family headed to the island to escape the rigors of the post-election frenzy. George and Barbara joined the family for the trip, as did Columba and Jeb who planned "to do some golfing and fishing, and relaxing, and I'm sure he's probably reading e-mails as well," Jeb's press secretary told *The Miami Herald*.

While in Boca Grande, the family often resides at the Gasparilla Inn, a resort known for upper-class clientele. During these island vacations, the President and his family have a chance to enjoy some of the fishing, golfing and tennis for which the island is known. "The Bush family is very low-key," remarked local newspaper journalist Gary Dutery in an article that appeared in *The Orlando Sentinel*. "They mostly travel around on golf carts."

Home Sweet Home

While George W. Bush's lifestyle may not be that different from many other Americans, his home certainly is. The new president

AP/WWP

recently traded in his elegant home at the Texas governor's mansion for the prestigious living quarters of the White House.

While Laura Bush has not discussed her plans yet, the nation has been busy speculating on how

First Lady Laura Bush will have the honor of decorating the White House and making it feel like home for her and George W.

she will choose to decorate her new home. Laura met with former First Lady Hillary Clinton in December 2000 for the ceremonial tea and an official tour of the White House, but the daughter-in-law of former president George Bush needed no introduction to the building where her in-laws resided for four years. "I feel like I sort of know it," Laura was reported to have said. "I have slept in the Lincoln Bedroom, and the Queen's Bedroom."

George W. built this ranch house that sits on 1,600 acres of lush Texas soil as a second residence for his family.

George W. and Laura also recently bought Prairie Chapel, a 1,600-acre ranch in Crawford, Texas, where they have built a single-level ranch-style home. "I loved the variety of the land," he told reporters who toured his complex in July 2000. "It's a unique place that's got a lot of Texas to it." While most of the land is dusty and barren, Bush has recently added a swimming pool (at his daughters' request, according to *Time* magazine) and a man-made 10-acre pond stocked with bass. President Bush will make this his new "home away from home," during the next four years and is delighted with the progress of the ranch, which he calls his "little slice of heaven."

Residents of the tiny town of Crawford are excited about what the new first family's residency has done for them. It has put Crawford on the map, as the town has been mentioned in newspapers and magazines, as well as on national television and radio. Property values are expected to skyrocket and new businesses may flock into town. Some residents are even hoping that the bumpy roads – one of the towns-people's biggest complaints – will soon be fixed.

In fact, President Bush's new residence has already become a "hot spot" among tourists and new regulations have been put in place for the protection of the state's former governor and his family. Perhaps, George should take a hint from his parents, who had a law passed in Texas to "regulate and restrict access to streets, avenues, alleys and boulevards in the municipality on which the dwelling of a former president of the United States is located."

Kennebunkport: Home Away From Home

The Bush family has long been associated with Kennebunkport, Maine, where former President George Bush and his family have spent their vacations at Walker's Point. Located on the Atlantic Ocean, the 26-room mansion has been in the family for several generations, ever since George's grandfather, George Herbert Walker, built the home in 1903. The former President spent his summers there as a boy and continues to use the

The Bush's vacation home on Walker's Point in Kennebunkport, Maine.

mansion as a summer home and home base for family gatherings. It has been the location for many Bush holidays and reunions.

The grandchildren come to visit nearly every summer. "Last summer we brought home 12 grandkids after the convention," Barbara told PEOPLE magazine in 2000. "They go to the beach. They boat, play tennis and swim for hours."

Most of them are all grown up, but at one time the Bush children needed to hold Grandma's and Grandpa's hands as they walked the grounds of Walker's Point.

Daily Life

Over the next four years, you may see a lot of similarities between George W. Bush and his famous father. Besides the physical resemblance, the two men share similar work ethics and habits.

Like his father (and working Americans all around the country), George W. Bush has a routine that maps out his day. The president rises early (usually between 6 a.m. and 7 a.m.), feeds the cats, walks the dog and then brings coffee and the newspaper back to his wife,

Laura, in bed. He works throughout the morning, but takes a break in the afternoon for his daily jog.

George Bush followed a similar routine, while in office, waking early and then enjoying coffee and the daily newspaper in bed with Barbara. He also was an avid jogger; it was one of the many athletic passions he held while in the White House.

And speaking of athletics, friendly competitions are as much of a Bush family tradition as vacationing. Whether it be golf, tennis or horseshoes, the Bush men are always up to the challenge. Marvin has been said to be the best athlete of the bunch, although his father, brothers and even brother-in-law Bobby Koch rise to the competition!

George W. isn't the only one to be following in his parents' footsteps into the White House. Spot Fletcher, the Bush family dog, is the offspring of Millie, George and Barbara's English springer spaniel who entertained the nation with her antics during George's presidency. Spot was actually born in the White House and is sure to be enjoying the return to his birthplace and his newfound status as the nation's "top dog."

Although members of the Bush family are spread across the nation, they stay in touch with one another by phone. With many impressive locations at which to gather, you can bet that the next four years will be filled with the delights that come with a large family: humorous anecdotes, regular reunions and lots of laughs!

Reuters NewMedia Inc./CORBIS

A picture-perfect moment – Barbara takes a photo of (l-r) family friends Bill and Will Farish and George W. and Jeb while rounding the golf course on Gasparilla Island, Florida.

The Next Generation Of Bushes

As George W. Bush takes his position as president of the United States, many eyes have turned with curiosity to the next generation of the Bush clan. Although many of the younger Bushes, such as Jeb Jr., Walker and Ashley (grandchildren of former president George Bush), are still too young to spend much time in the public eye, several of the Bush grandchildren have already begun to make their presence felt in the world at large.

Lauren Bush, the daughter of Neil and Sharon, has been modeling since she was 13 years old, and has appeared in several fashion magazines such as *W* and *Vogue*, as well as in an Abercrombie & Fitch advertising campaign. Although for the time being, Lauren professes to not be interested in following in her famous family's political footsteps, her mother Sharon knows that anything is possible. "If you grow up around politics, it's a part of you," she has said. If she

George Bush keeps an eye on two of his grandsons, Pierce (left) and Walker Bush (right), as the 2000 convention comes to a close.

does decide to go into politics, Lauren already has a good start in foreign relations – she and Prince William of Great Britain have reportedly been e-mail pals for the last few years.

Lauren's younger brother Pierce is another Bush who has attracted interest as of late. He made quite an impression on media types at the 2000 Republican National Convention. Journalists were impressed with his poise, charisma and natural affinity for the spotlight. It may be too soon to tell what the future holds for young Pierce, but as a veteran of three GOP conventions and nationally televised interviews, Pierce is clearly learning his way around the political arena.

Perhaps the most talked-about member of the younger Bush generation is George Prescott Bush, the twenty-something son of Florida governor Jeb Bush. "P.," as he is called by family and friends, burst onto the political scene during his uncle George W.'s presidential campaign. A law student at the University of Texas (the same school his cousin Jenna attends as an undergraduate), he helped attract both Hispanics and young people to the Republican party with his savvy sound bites, movie star good looks and the ease with which he addressed large and small groups alike. Referred to by some as the Bushes' "secret weapon," he repeatedly stated that he does not intend to go into politics. However, given his performance during the campaign and his dedication to public service, some feel that he could be an up-and-coming star in the political world if he so chose. For now, he is concentrating on his law studies, preparing to become the first lawyer in the Bush family.

His bilingual address to the nation put George P. on the political map and in the hearts of young female Republicans everywhere.

And what of George W. Bush's children? So far, the president's twin daughters, Barbara and Jenna, have shown no desire to get involved in politics. During their father's campaign, they purposely stayed far out of the spotlight and are focusing on their college careers. Barbara, however, is in one way already following the Bush family path. She is a student at Yale University, an institution her father, grandfather and great-grandfather attended before launching their political careers.

Besides these impressive young people, there are several other Bushes waiting in the wings, including Jeb Bush's twenty-something daughter Noelle, as well as Marvin's and Dorothy's children. Given the legacy their family members have forged before them, we would not be surprised to see Bushes dotting the political landscape for a long time to come.

Meet The Bushes

Now that the election hoopla has passed and the Inaugural Ball has come and gone, George W. Bush is settling down to his duties as president and the United States is getting to know a new first family. George W. is the second Bush to hold the highest office in the land, and members of the Bush family have now held elected office for three generations. Who are the members of our newest political dynasty and how did they get where they are today?

The following section answers these questions as we profile the more than 30 members of the extended Bush clan, from the great-grandfather of the president all the way to the youngest member of the Bush family. In between, you'll glimpse into the lives of President Bush, First Lady Laura Bush and their twin daughters, Jenna and Barbara. We'll also introduce you to President Bush's siblings and their children, some of whom are already causing talk of a whole new generation of Bush politicians.

George Bush plays with Neil's kids (from left) Ashley, Lauren and Pierce in 1989.

Keep reading for an intimate look into the lives of this tight-knit clan. You'll learn what drives the Bushes, and what keeps them together. You'll learn about old traditions and favorite pastimes. Trace the rise of a political dynasty and decide for yourself which Bush is next in line for political glory.

We also provide personal information such as birth dates, hometowns, marital status and more! So turn the page and get ready to take an intimate peek inside one of America's most fascinating families.

George W. Bush

43rd President
of the United States

★ WHO IS GEORGE W. BUSH ANYWAY? The son of former president George Bush, George W. served two terms as governor of Texas and is currently the 43rd president of the United States.

Full Name
George Walker Bush

Birth Date
July 6, 1946

Birthplace
New Haven, Connecticut

Resides
Washington, D.C.

What's He Up To?
43rd president
of the United States

Marital Status
Married to
Laura Welch Bush

Children
Barbara and Jenna

As he enters the White House, George W. Bush, now in his mid-50s, has experienced a number of key turning points that have defined the man we see today.

The Early Years

George W.'s roots are in the Northeast, where he was born on July 6, 1946 in New Haven, Connecticut. His father, former President George Bush, was a Yale University student at the time. After graduation, George W.'s father decided to take his wife and young son to Texas, to strike out on his own in the oil business.

The young family eventually came to the town of Midland, in the heart of the West Texas oil country. George W. grew to adolescence in Midland, a town that had a profound effect in shaping his character. He was the oldest of six children – Robin (who died of leukemia in 1953 at the age of three), John (nicknamed Jeb), Neil, Marvin and Dorothy.

Robin's death had a sobering effect on the family and George W. took it upon himself to cheer up his parents. The young boy often chose to stay at home rather than spend time playing with friends. Family and humor became two values that would stick with George W. and help shape him into the man he is today.

George W. spent a great deal of his time at Yale on the playing fields.

George W. went to public school in Midland where he was a popular student at San Jacinto Junior High. For high school, however, his parents decided to send him to the prestigious Phillips Academy in Andover, Massachusetts, the same prep school his father had attended.

Which George?

With all the men named "George Bush" in the Bush family, it can be hard to keep them straight. In this book, "George W." is the current president, "George" is the former president and "George P." is Jeb Bush's son.

Although he once described the school as "cold and distant and difficult," George W. was popular there and surrounded himself with a close group of friends. In addition to playing basketball and baseball, he appointed himself "high commissioner" of stickball.

After Phillips Academy, George W. followed in his father's footsteps and earned a bachelor's degree from Yale in 1968. The Vietnam War was at its peak

George Bush Presidential Library

at this time and he felt he had to play a role in the military, lest it hurt his father's political image – the elder Bush was serving as a first-term U.S. congressman representing a Houston-area district. So George W. enlisted in a pilot training program of the Texas Air National Guard. He rose to the rank of lieu-

From left, George W., George P., Jeb and Laura Bush wave hello as they arrive in West Palm Beach, Florida, for a campaign rally.

tenant and entered the Reserves, but he was never sent to Vietnam.

During this time, George W. became more and more frustrated with his life. As his father moved up the political ranks, George felt as though he would never live up to his father's grand achievements. His frustrations led him into a life of partying hard and accomplishing little.

Career Highlights

Although George W. was in the oil business in the 1970s and early 1980s, his first major business success came in 1989, when he and a group of partners purchased the Texas Rangers baseball team. His role as managing general partner propelled him into the spotlight and, arguably, helped to pave the way for his successful run for governor of Texas in 1994.

George And Laura

The next stop for George W. was Harvard Business School, where he earned an M.B.A. in 1975. Upon graduation, he returned to Midland and, like his father before him, founded his own oil exploration company. It was during this period that he was introduced to Laura Welch, an elementary school librarian, at a dinner at the home of mutual friends. George W. was instantly enamored with her – it was love at first sight. Laura was the per-

The Greek Years

While a student at Yale University, George W. was president of his fraternity, Delta Kappa Epsilon.

George Bush Presidential Library

The proud father of newborn twins, George W. cradles his daughters soon after their birth in 1981.

fect match for George. A reserved woman, her calm demeanor tempered George's wild side. Just by saying his nickname, "Bushie," she could get him to settle down when his emotions were getting the best of him. They were married in a small ceremony just three months later.

By all accounts, they have a happy, loving and supportive relationship. George W. has said, "No matter what else I do in life, asking Laura to marry me was the best decision I ever made."

The Midland Blues

The young couple soon found things did not always go their way. When the seat in th U.S. Congress representing the Midland area became vacant, George W. entered the race. He won the Republican primary, but lost the general election.

Even trying to have a child did not result in quick success. But after three years of trying, Laura Bush became pregnant and gave birth to twin daughters, Barbara Pierce and Jenna Welch.

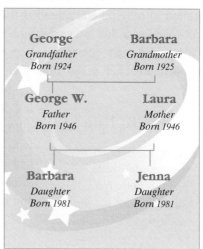

Family Tree

George	Barbara
Grandfather	*Grandmother*
Born 1924	*Born 1925*

George W.	Laura
Father	*Mother*
Born 1946	*Born 1946*

Barbara	Jenna
Daughter	*Daughter*
Born 1981	*Born 1981*

Bagging The Elephant

The 1970s were a booming period for the oil industry, but when it came to "bagging the elephant" (slang for striking oil), George W.'s company came up short. The fact that oil prices started to decline in the 1980s, making it harder to obtain investment capital, didn't help matters.

George and Laura pose with daughters Barbara (left) and Jenna (right).

In 1984, George W. merged his company with another small oil exploration company, and he took over as chairman of the new concern. Business did not improve.

Confronting His Troubles

Throughout his business troubles, George W. continued to struggle with excessive drinking, a problem that was beginning to hurt those around him. His path back to a healthy lifestyle began when he turned to religion and attended Bible studies regularly. At a family get-together at his father's summer home in Kennebunkport, Maine, George W. met celebrated evangelist Billy Graham. When the famous preacher asked him, "Are you right with God?" George replied, "No, but I want to be." A turning point came in 1986 after a drunken 40th birthday celebration. He awoke with a bad hangover and decided he'd had enough of drinking. He doesn't drink at all, even socially, to this day and he openly discusses his faith.

Fit To Run

George W. is an avid jogger who made sure to schedule time for exercise into his busy campaigning schedule.

Bush, Texas Ranger

No longer an owner of the Texas Rangers, Bush sold his share of the franchise in 1998 for a reported $14 million.

AP/WWP

Though he gave up his position as managing general partner of the Texas Rangers, George still cheers for his team, as seen here during a September 1994 game against the California Angels.

Baseball And Politics

Business life began to improve for George W. in 1984 as well. He sold his company to the Harken Energy Corporation in exchange for stock, which he later sold for a substantial profit. He also remained on the Harken payroll as a consultant for several years.

After his turn in the oil business, George W. got some valuable political experience working as an advisor on his father's successful presidential campaign in 1988. An oft-repeated story is that after his father became president, George W. asked White House aide Doug Wead, "So, what do I do now?" Wead, a meticulous researcher, came up with a 44-page memo titled "All The President's Children." His findings showed that first family offspring historically had "higher than average rates of alcoholism, divorce, suicide and lost opportunities," and that "no presidential son had ever been elected governor in American history." When he read the memo, George W. is said to have lamented, "Oh, great."

He Did It His Way

George W. has said that his successful career as owner of the Texas Rangers gave him credibility with voters. In his first season as owner, he told reporters, "It solved my biggest political problem in Texas. My problem was, 'What's the boy ever done?'"

He may have taken the memo as a wake-up call, however, as his life has been marked by determination and success ever since.

When the Texas Rangers baseball team was put up for sale in 1989, George W.

George W. and vice presidential candidate Dick Cheney get up close and personal with their supporters at a campaign rally.

wanted to buy in and quickly organized a group of local investors who bought the franchise. He was chosen to serve as managing general partner and the team prospered under George W.'s ownership.

Governor Bush

In 1993, George W. decided to make a second stab at elected office, announcing his candidacy for governor of Texas. George easily won the GOP nomination, setting him up to take on popular incumbent governor Ann Richards, who was seeking re-election. The tart-tongued Richards was famous for once having described George W.'s father as having been born "with a silver foot in his mouth" and enjoyed referring to George W. as "Shrub." Taking the high road, Bush chose not to return the "compliments" and instead stressed what he considered to be his best issues – education, welfare reform and tougher juvenile justice laws.

With his easy smile and quick wit, George easily pulled off a victory in November 1994 and became only the second Republican to be elected Texas

Home On The Range

Although Kennebunkport, Maine is still the place where the Bush clan typically gathers, George W. has built a sprawling ranch near Crawford, Texas, where he and his family go to relax.

governor since the post-Civil War reconstruction era. Four years later, George W. became the first Texas governor to be re-elected to a second consecutive term.

George W.'s years as Texas governor were marked by the same humor that has endeared him to his fans all over the United States. With a sparkle in his eye, he would tease friends, family and staff. He dressed comfortably (often in jeans and cowboy boots), spent his spare time reading or enjoying time with his family and never tried to be something other than the down-home country boy from Midland that he is. A likable, but intense, man, those who knew him realized that George W.'s political career would not stop at the Texas Governor's Mansion.

Laura and George Bush (left) join Dick and Lynne Cheney (right) on stage at the grand finale of the Republican National Convention held in Philadelphia on August 3, 2000.

The Presidential Race

Not long after his second gubernatorial win, George W. announced he would seek his party's nomination for president for the year 2000. He quickly became the choice of his party and had little trouble raising campaign funds.

George W. won the presidency, though it was several weeks after election day until the results were finalized. He took office on January 20, 2001, and, as he assumes the role of 43rd president, George W. carries the Bush political tradition into a new millennium.

APWWP

Laura
Bush

Wife
of the president

★ Who Is Laura Bush Anyway? Wife of President George W. Bush, Laura Bush is the first lady of the United States. She is the mother of twin girls, Jenna and Barbara, and is devoted to championing the causes of literacy and education.

Full Name
Laura Welch Bush

Birth Date
November 4, 1946

Birthplace
Midland, Texas

Resides
Washington, D.C.

What's She Up To?
First Lady
of the United States

Marital Status
Married to
George W. Bush

Children
Barbara and Jenna

Former First Lady Barbara Bush likes to tell the story of when Laura Bush was first introduced to her husband's grandmother (former President George Bush's mother Dorothy Walker Bush). Barbara Bush described the now-deceased Dorothy as perhaps "the most athletic human being living." Upon being introduced to her grandson's future wife, Dorothy asked Laura, "What do you do?" When Laura replied, "I read," Barbara Bush says Dorothy couldn't believe her ears, and she "darn near collapsed."

Opposites Do Attract

Laura and George W. Bush may well be an example of the proverbial opposites attracting. One friend of the couple puts it this way: "George is always bouncing off the walls" while Laura, on the other hand, "is so quiet." Laura Bush herself is quick to recognize advantages in their contrasting personalities. She says she tempers his brashness, while he has made life much more exciting for her.

George Bush Presidential Library

Laura and George W. beam on their wedding day.

Though his wife's personality may differ from his, George W. Bush is quick to praise her unique qualities, "She cuts right through the posturing and positioning," he has said. "America's starved for something . . . they're starved for something real. And that's what she brings. She's a real person."

A few months younger than her husband, Laura was born in Midland, Texas, the same town in which her future husband grew up and later ran an oil exploration company. She is the only child of Harold Welch, a homebuilder, and his wife, Jenna, who worked as his bookkeeper. Her home life as a child has been described as loving and happy.

Do I Know You?

Although the whole world knows her now, when she was the first lady of Texas Laura Bush still had a degree of anonymity. One time, while shopping in a Wal-Mart, a woman in the checkout line chatted with Laura and her two daughters. She thought Laura looked familiar, but could not put her finger on how she knew her. When she heard her name was Laura Bush, the woman had to say sorry, but that name just did not ring a bell. It must now!

A Twist Of Fate

Laura and George W. attended different elementary schools but went to the same junior high school for seventh grade, although they didn't really know each other at the time. George subsequently went off to the prestigious Phillips Academy prep school in Andover, Massachusetts, while Laura attended a local Midland high school. Her high school years were marred by a tragic auto accident that ended fatally for one of the parties involved.

Laura had been an excellent student in high school, and there was no doubt that she would be pursuing higher education. Laura's parents, who hadn't finished college, had put money aside for her schooling from the time she was very young and were able to send her to Southern Methodist University in Dallas. Laura, who as a little girl used to practice teaching to a "class" made up of her dolls, majored in education.

Laura and George W. have enjoyed more than 25 years of marital bliss.

A few years later, when feminism became part of the culture, Laura once complained to her father that he shouldn't have "programmed" her to be a teacher. Maybe she could have been a lawyer, she said. Her surprised father pulled out his wallet and offered to send her to law school. At that point, she laughingly admitted that she didn't want to be a lawyer – she wanted to teach.

After graduation, she taught elementary school for three years, first in Dallas and then in Houston, where her path could have crossed her future husband's, as they lived in the same apartment complex, but they never met. Which may have been just as well, since that was during George W.'s alleged "wilder" days when he served in the Texas Air National Guard.

Laura went on to earn her master's degree in library science and then worked as an elementary school librarian in Austin, Texas. By 1977, George was in the oil business and living in Midland. When Laura went home for a visit, a Midland couple who were mutual friends invited them over for a barbecue. George later described it as love at

Meet The Parents

George and Barbara Bush appreciate their daughter-in-law's quiet strength and reserve. George has referred to her as the "Rock of Gibraltar." Barbara says Laura is unflappable, "in contrast to our family, which is anything but calm."

first sight, while Laura said, "I don't know that it was love at first sight, but it was pretty close." Whatever the case, three months later they were married. As a condition, Laura made him promise she would never have to give a political speech.

It was only a matter of months before that promise went by the wayside as George made his first foray into politics, when he ran unsuccessfully for

Join The Club

Laura loves to read, and while living in Texas, was a member of a book club.

Congress. "That's how it goes with political promises," she later said, jokingly. Laura worked full-time on the campaign and describes that effort as having drawn the couple very close.

Both Laura, who had given up her career when they were married, and George wanted to have children early in the marriage, but it was three years before Laura would become pregnant, and they were actually beginning the process of adoption at the time. In what is the

George Bush Presidential Library

Bushes' version of "two for the price of one," Laura gave birth to fraternal twin girls, named Barbara and Jenna. The pregnancy had been difficult, as Laura had developed toxemia, a potentially life-threatening condition. As the toxemia grew more severe, her doctors decided to deliver the twins early by cesarean section. George W. has said, "She loves our daughters more than anything, she would lay her life down for them

Barbara, George, Jenna and Laura (left to right) show their all-American colors during the summer of 1991.

and nearly did at birth." Later, when asked what she wanted people to know about her, the first thing she would say is that she's a mother of twin girls. She has by all accounts been a mother who is very devoted to, and protective of, her children.

Taking To The Campaign Trail

Drawing on her earlier experience with her husband's campaign, Laura participated alongside her husband in her father-in-law's successful 1988 presidential campaign, as well as the unsuccessful one four years later. Those experiences served to draw her closer to the large Bush clan. She became especially close to her mother-in-law, Barbara Bush, whom she describes as "a terrific role model for any woman . . . very independent, very strong, irreverent and lots of fun."

George W. takes Laura and Spot Fletcher for a tour of their new home in Crawford, Texas, in July 2000.

Because of her experiences in George Bush's 1992 campaign, she was somewhat concerned when George W. decided to give the political life another shot by running for Texas governor in 1994. She says, "I just wanted George to think about it, make sure it was really what he wanted."

The First Lady

He was elected, and as Texas' first lady, Laura Bush championed the cause of literacy, especially for children. During her tenure she promoted early learning programs which prepare children to read at an early age. She also founded the Texas Book Festival, which has attracted many prominent authors and helped raise nearly a million dollars for the state's public libraries. She was also very active in breast cancer awareness programs.

How Times Change

Laura initially resisted meeting George W. fearing that "he was someone I wouldn't be interested in because I was so uninterested in politics at that time."

Given her initial aversion to making speeches, it is probably safe to assume that Laura Bush never dreamed that she would be called upon, at age 53, to address a political party national convention during prime time. But that's what happened on July 31, 2000, at the GOP convention in Philadelphia. After congratulating the party on its choice of a nominee, she talked about a personal passion – the importance of education and reading.

Laura Bush, who is committed to the cause of literacy, reads to third graders at a school in Flowood, Mississippi.

She then went on to say in her speech, "George and I grew up in Midland, Texas – a small town in a vast desert – a place where neighbors had to help each other because any other help was too far away. Midland was a place of family and community, and it had a sense of possibility as big as the West Texas sky. Midland formed value reserves as deep and longer lasting than any of its oil wells."

Good Books

Some of the books that Mrs. Bush, a former elementary school librarian, suggests that parents and their children read together are *The Little House On The Prairie* series, by Laura Ingalls Wilder, *Charlotte's Web*, by E.B. White and *Little Women*, by Louisa May Alcott.

As first lady, she plans to promote literacy and education programs similar to those she championed in Texas. When asked if she would be more like Barbara Bush or Hillary Clinton, she replied, "I think I'll just be like Laura Bush." If past successes are any indication of things to come, that should be quite enough.

APWWP

Barbara
Bush

Daughter
of the president

★ WHO IS BARBARA BUSH ANYWAY? Barbara is the older of George W.'s twin daughters, and is considered to be quieter and more studious than her sister. She is currently a student at Yale University and she and her sister Jenna represent the first time that twins are part of a "first family."

Full Name
Barbara Pierce Bush

Birth Date
November 25, 1981

Birthplace
Dallas

Resides
Crawford, Texas

What's She Up To?
Student at Yale University

Marital Status
Single

Despite her starring role as "first daughter" in George W. Bush's presidency, Barbara is not likely to step into the spotlight any time soon. This unassuming student will be doing her best to stay out of the public eye while she's attending college.

Stars From The Start

Born five weeks prematurely on November 25, 1981, fraternal twins Barbara and Jenna Bush arrived right in the midst of their grandfather's term as vice president. Each of the twins was named after one of their grandmothers – Barbara was named for the former first lady.

Because of their famous family, the twins were immediately thrust into the pub-

Guess Who?

In the past, Barbara has been known to don such Halloween costumes as a bunch of grapes and as "Vampora" the vampire.

lic eye, holding their very first "press conference" just two hours after they were born. Since then, however, their parents have been very protective of the young women and have asked that the news media not pry into their lives.

Double Trouble

Though *most* of the time they were well-behaved little girls, Barbara and her sister still got involved in their fair share of childhood

George Bush Presidential Library

pranks. On a flight from Texas to Washington, on the day after their grandfather was elected president, they managed to clog up an airplane toilet with paper. Their down-to-earth grandmother, Barbara Bush, later wrote, "I was up to my elbows pulling it out."

Another time, while staying with their grandparents, Barbara and Jenna announced that they were supposed to be in bed at

Barbara (left) and Jenna (right) Bush at age 7.

9:30 p.m. A quick phone call to George W. and Laura revealed that the girls actually had a bedtime of 8:30 p.m. "You should've seen their faces caught in the act, both of them," wrote George Bush in his autobiography. "They are so cute . . ."

Split Personality

In the fall of 2000, Barbara entered the Yale University class of 2004. As such, she carries on a family tradition, becoming the fourth consecutive generation to attend the Ivy League school. At Yale, the undergrads each belong to one of 12 residential colleges, and Barbara chose Davenport College, the one to which both her father and grandfather belonged. During the summer before her freshman year, Barbara joined many fellow incoming freshman for four days of hiking and camping on the Appalachian Trail.

Jenna (center) and Barbara Bush (right) embrace their father after his acceptance speech at the 2000 Republican National Convention.

But just because Barbara hits the books doesn't mean she doesn't like to have fun. Among her high school accomplishments is having been named homecoming queen at Stephen F. Austin High School, a public school in the Texas capital. Barbara also participated in sports, including softball. And proving that she's not just about books and studying, Barbara was voted "most likely to appear on the cover of *Vogue*" by her fellow classmates.

Considering the past achievements of Barbara's family, and the groundwork she's already laid out for herself, there seems to be little doubt that Barbara will make the best of her education, and the experiences she's afforded, and go on to make a considerable mark in the world.

Puppy Love

Barbara holds the distinction of having named the Bush family's puppy (who now has the title of "first dog") Spot Fletcher. The dog is named after Barbara's then-favorite baseball player, former Texas Rangers infielder Scott Fletcher. Spot is an offspring of Barbara's grandparents' dog, the well-known former "first dog," Millie.

Jenna
Bush

AP/WWP

Daughter
of the president

★ WHO IS JENNA BUSH ANYWAY? Jenna is the younger of George W.'s twin daughters, and the one who is frequently described as the more outgoing of the two. She is currently a student at the University of Texas at Austin.

Despite the huge role her family has taken in politics, "first daughter" Jenna Bush has been able to enjoy life as a regular American teenager.

An Early Arrival

Jenna and her twin sister, Barbara, were born prematurely in Dallas, Texas, on November 25, 1981, with Jenna being the second to arrive. Jenna weighed only 4 pounds, 12 ounces and was named for her maternal grandmother – Jenna Welch.

Standing Apart

Jenna is a graduate of Stephen F. Austin High School, a public school in Austin, Texas, where she demonstrated an early interest in politics. While there, she served

Full Name
Jenna Welch Bush

Birth Date
November 25, 1981

Birthplace
Dallas

Resides
Crawford, Texas

What's She Up To?
Student at the
University of Texas

Marital Status
Single

on the student council and was elected vice president of her senior class.

As a reporter for her high school's newspaper, Jenna didn't shy away from tackling tough issues. In one story, Jenna commented on an incident where local police raided a party that included underage drinking. While the police found many white kids with beers in their hands, she wrote, "The cops headed directly for the only black person in sight."

Of the two girls, Jenna is often considered the more outgoing. Her friends at school called her "doughnut girl" because she

A jubilant Jenna Bush receives her high school diploma from Stephen F. Austin High School.

could always be counted on to provide snacks. And Jenna proved that she was tough enough to withstand a little friendly ribbing when the members of the senior class voted her "most likely to trip on prom night." (Though she didn't.)

When she entered the freshman class in 2000, Jenna became one of nearly 50,000 students at the University of Texas at Austin. She's not the first presidential daughter to attend the University of Texas – Lyndon Baines Johnson's daughter, Lynda, also attended the Texas institution.

Did She Really Say That?

Jenna is not afraid to tell her father what she thinks, much to his chagrin. She has been quoted as saying that her father isn't "half as cool as people think." The Bush family believes that Jenna has a flair for being outspoken just like her grandmother, Barbara, the former first lady.

"Oh, Dad!"

Jenna, who's notoriously camera-shy, might credit her instincts to the embarrassing situations her father has

A proud Jenna Bush applauds her mother Laura during her speech at the 2000 Republican National Convention.

unintentionally put her in. One such incident occurred during the lighting of the family's Christmas tree in 1994. Her father had just been elected governor of Texas, and the press had been invited to cover the family's ritual tree trimming. During the event, the phone rang, and Jenna's dad wondered aloud if the caller might be a young man who was interested in his daughter. To make matters worse, he even gave the boy's name to the press!

Another such event occurred recently when George revealed to the press that Jenna's boyfriend was a pitcher on the high school baseball team. This also raised Jenna's ire, for he later said: "Boy did I hear about that the next morning. It's the last personal story I tell about [Jenna], I'll tell you that."

The Future

When all is said and done, it's rather obvious that the Bushes would prefer that whatever attention Jenna gets will be based on her own accomplishments. As a student attending a first-rate college, that will in all likelihood be the case for Jenna in the many years to come.

What A Way To Spend Christmas!

On Christmas night, 2000, Jenna made headlines when she was rushed to St. David's Hospital in Austin, Texas, complaining of abdominal pains. She was quickly diagnosed with appendicitis and underwent an emergency appendectomy. Her surgery was deemed a success and she made a speedy recovery.

Robin
Bush

Sister
of the president

Pauline Robinson Bush (known as "Robin" to friends and family) was born on December 20, 1949. She died of leukemia on October 11, 1953. Although Robin's life lasted just less than four years, she had an unforgettable impact on all who met her.

Although they never got over her death, George and Barbara eventually learned to cherish their memories of Robin. "We still miss our Robin," George wrote a few years after Robin's death. "At times Bar and I each find ourselves vividly recalling the beauty and charm of our little girl."

Barbara has also told of the impact Robin's death has had on her. In her memoirs, she wrote, "George and I love and value every person more because of Robin. She lives on in our hearts, memories, actions, and through the Bright Star Foundation [a foundation for leukemia research the Bushes started in Robin's memory]."

In honor of Robin, George and Barbara have been active in aiding leukemia research. George explained his feelings about the tragedy in his autobiography, when he said, "To this day, like every parent who has ever lost a child, we wonder why; yet we know that, whatever the reason, she is in God's loving arms."

Family Tree

	George	Barbara			
	Father *Born 1924*	*Mother* *Born 1925*			
George W.	**Robin**	**Jeb**	**Neil**	**Marvin**	**Dorothy**
Son *Born 1946*	*Daughter* *1949-1953*	*Son* *Born 1953*	*Son* *Born 1955*	*Son* *Born 1956*	*Daughter* *Born 1959*

Jeb
Bush

AP/WWP

Brother
of the president

★ **WHO IS JEB BUSH ANYWAY?** John Ellis "Jeb" Bush was one of two Bushes to become governor of a large southern state. He had careers in banking and real estate development before he made the plunge into politics.

Jeb Bush is no stranger to close calls. He lost the Florida election for governor in 1994 by one of the narrowest margins in Florida history. He vowed to firm up his political agenda and ran again in 1998, and that time the outcome was a success. Little did he know that two years later, in 2000, Florida would become embroiled in the most bizarre presidential election in history.

The Early Years

Jeb, the governor formally known as John Ellis Bush, is the second oldest son of George and Barbara Bush and was born on February 11, 1953.

He attended the Phillips Academy as a high school student, during which time he

Full Name
John Ellis "Jeb" Bush

Birth Date
February 11, 1953

Birthplace
Midland, Texas

Resides
Tallahassee, Florida

What's He Up To?
Governor of Florida

Marital Status
Married to Columba Bush

Children
George P., Noelle
and Jeb Jr.

George Bush Presidential Library

Three generations of Bushes pose in this 1984 photograph
(clockwise from left: Jeb holding Jeb Jr., George, Barbara, Columba, George P. and Noelle).

traveled to Mexico as an exchange student. There, he met and fell in love with a young local woman, Columba Garnica Gallo. Jeb and Columba began courting through letters and visited each other as often as possible.

After high school, Jeb moved on to the University of Texas and went on to graduate with a bachelor's degree in Latin American Studies. Upon graduating, he and Columba married on February 23,

Sibling Rivalry

It was generally thought that Jeb would be the first of former president George Bush's sons to hold public office. But it was actually his older brother, George W. Bush, who became the first to hold office by being elected governor of the state of Texas.

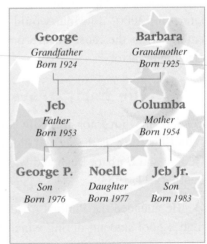

Family Tree

George	Barbara
Grandfather	*Grandmother*
Born 1924	*Born 1925*

Jeb	Columba
Father	*Mother*
Born 1953	*Born 1954*

George P.	Noelle	Jeb Jr.
Son	*Daughter*	*Son*
Born 1976	*Born 1977*	*Born 1983*

For More Info

To contact Jeb Bush or to read his weekly "Governor's Message," log on to *www.state.fl.us* or e-mail the governor at *fl_governor@eog.state.fl.us*

AP/WWP

A governor's job is never done! Here, Jeb Bush checks his E-mail during some personal time.

Career Highlights

1998-Present
Governor of Florida

1987-1988
Florida Commerce Secretary

1984-1986
Dade County (FL)
Republican Chairman

1981
Co-founder of Codina Group, a real estate development firm

1974
Vice President of the Texas Commerce Bank branch in Caracas, Venezuela

1974. Jeb then put his degree to good use when he relocated to Caracas, Venezuela, to work as a vice president of the Texas Commerce Bank.

Jeb Lands In Florida

After his stay in South America, Jeb moved to Miami. Teaming up with Armando Codina, a young Jeb founded the Codina Group, a real estate development company. He also served as the Dade County Republican chairman from 1984-1986 and became Florida Commerce Secretary from 1987-1988.

A Run For Governor

In 1994, Jeb ran for governor of Florida and faced a tough fight against Democratic incumbent Lawton Chiles. Jeb was seen as a conservative extremist by some; someone who was not concerned with the problems of women and minorities in the state. He eventually lost his bid for the governorship – 49% of the vote went to Bush, while 51% went to Chiles – in what was one of the closest gubernatorial races ever in Florida.

The Second Time's A Charm

When Jeb ran for governor in 1998, he took a stronger stand on education and cultural diversity. Concerned about the state's poverty levels, Jeb showed he cared by taking on the lifetime commitment of being the godfather to a poor African-American boy. In a move to

AP/WWP

increase the quality of education within impoverished areas, Jeb set up the Liberty City Charter School to assist underprivileged kids in the Miami area.

Jeb campaigned in the poor and decimated areas of the state, as well as in Democratic strongholds in South

Jeb Bush and his brother George W. Bush joke around during a bus ride to a November 2000 rally at Florida International University.

Florida's retirement communities. This time, he won the election over incumbent Lieutenant Governor Buddy MacKay. With Jeb's victory, the Bush brothers became the first simultaneous sibling governors since Nelson and Winthrop Rockefeller in the 1960s.

Did You Know?

Florida governor Lawton Chiles died soon before Jeb Bush was sworn in as his successor. Chiles had beaten Bush in a close election in 1994, but couldn't run again in 1998 because of Florida term limits.

Rising Star On The National Scene

Jeb Bush was already considered a rising star in the Republican Party long before his brother decided to run for the presidency, and the 2000 election campaign catapulted Jeb into an even higher national profile. The early years of his term as the governor of Florida were marked by his crusades for education (including a controversial school vouchers program), tax cuts and issues regarding the environment. Some political observers speculate that Jeb Bush could someday launch his own campaign for president.

Jeb's son, George P. Bush, also became an instant celebrity during his uncle's campaign after delivering a speech at the Republican National Convention. Perhaps the Bush political roots will travel down this branch of the family next?

Election Controversy: So Many Chads, So Little Time

Jeb Bush as a toddler.

During election night coverage, Florida was originally given to Democratic candidate Al Gore, but the networks reviewed their decision and went on to give the state to Bush. Political observers had a field day with the fact that the 2000 presidential election wound up being decided in Jeb's home state of Florida. Jeb had promised his brother that he would help with the critical state and it could have been a real embarrassment for the Bushes if George W.'s razor-slim victory hadn't materialized. (It's anyone's guess if the post–Election Day controversies will affect Jeb Bush's political reputation.)

You Can Bank On It

Why did Jeb turn from banking to politics? Jeb quipped to the *St. Petersburg Times* that, "I wasn't really good at collecting loans."

Columba
Bush

Sister-In-Law
of the president

★ WHO IS COLUMBA BUSH ANYWAY? Mexican-born Columba is the wife of Jeb Bush, the governor of Florida. She is a passionate supporter of the arts, as well as anti-drug abuse programs.

Full Name
Columba Garnica
Gallo Bush

Birth Date
1954

Birthplace
Leon, Mexico

Resides
Tallahassee, Florida

What's She Up To?
Supports drug abuse
awareness organizations

Marital Status
Married to Jeb Bush

Children
George P., Noelle
and Jeb Jr.

As a child growing up in the central-Mexican town of Leon, young Columba (pronounced "Col-OOM-ba") Garnica Gallo probably didn't have a clue that one day she would marry into a high-profile American family, or that she'd become the first lady of Florida.

Young Love

Raised a devout Catholic in a single-parent home (her father left the family when she was 3 years old), Columba attended Catholic school with her two older siblings, Francisco and Lucila. She developed a passion for art and imagined that she would go on to lead a simple life in Mexico.

A Full House

Columba has two beloved pets – a chocolate Lab named Marvin and a bluepoint Siamese cat named Sugar.

It wasn't until 1971, when Columba was 16, and a tall, 17-year-old exchange student named Jeb Bush came to teach English at her school, that Columba's future seemed to expand. The 6-foot-4-inch Jeb fell deeply in love with Columba, who was a mere 5 feet tall (and, it is said, a little daunted by the boy's height), and soon she felt the same about her young suitor. After Jeb's visit was over, the couple spent three years exchanging letters and visiting whenever Jeb could fly to Mexico. Finally, on February 23, 1974, Columba married Jeb at the campus chapel of the University of Texas at Austin, in an English-language ceremony neither her mother nor her sister (who were both in attendance) could understand.

Columba's oldest son, George P. Bush, was very instrumental in George W. Bush's run for president.

A Growing Family

By 1980, Columba was the mother of two – George P. and Noelle – and she and Jeb moved to Miami, where their youngest son, Jeb Jr. (called "Jebby" by the family), would be born. In reverence to her childhood, Columba raised her children to be bilingual, and took them to Mass regularly. She threw herself into the parenting role while her husband built his career.

An Avid Reader

Like many of the Bushes, Columba loves to read in her spare time. She is especially fond of biographies, particularly books about opera singers and old-time movie stars such as Greta Garbo.

When that career flourished and Jeb became the governor of Florida in 1998, it was a confident and assured Columba who assumed the role of first lady. Soon after her husband took office, Columba began embarking on projects that were particularly important to her.

Matters Close To The Heart

Among Columba's most personal endeavors are drug-abuse prevention programs, especially those aimed at youngsters. One of her own children – she and Jeb decline to specify which one

Columba Bush greeting children during a Governor's Mansion ceremony.

– has struggled with drugs in the past. Now Columba spends a great deal of time with organizations such as Informed Families, which fights childhood drug abuse through family education. She is also involved with the Red Ribbon Foundation, an anti-drug organization which sponsors drug education programs in the Florida school system.

The arts are among Columba's other passions, one she says that can be used as a tool for inter-cultural understanding. She has co-founded the Children's Cultural Education Fund of Mexico's national dance troupe, Ballet Folklorico, in a move to bring free performances to U.S. school children (over 250,000 kids have seen the troupe since 1990), and she helps sponsor arts education and recognition programs all over the state of Florida.

Columba's Good Deeds

In addition to her anti-drug and arts-education work, Columba is also active in supporting Casa de la Amistad (literally, "friendship house"), a Mexican organization that provides a "home away from home" for the families of sick children who are receiving treatment at hospitals far from their homes.

George P. Bush

AP/WWP

Nephew
of the president

★ WHO IS GEORGE P. BUSH ANYWAY? The oldest son of Florida governor Jeb Bush and his wife Columba, George is a law student who created a splash during his uncle's 2000 presidential campaign.

He's been referred to as a cross between John F. Kennedy, Jr. and pop star Ricky Martin, and it's not hard to see why. As the late John Jr. did before him, George P. Bush – called "P." by his kin – has entered his famous family's political life with such ease and gusto that you'd think public graciousness was genetically encoded. Add to that his Ricky-esque perfect smile and Latino good looks and you've got material for *PEOPLE* magazine's "Top 100 Eligible Bachelors" issue – where, indeed, George P. showed up fourth on the 2000 list.

Full Name
George Prescott Bush

Birth Date
April 24, 1976

Birthplace
Houston

Resides
Austin, Texas

What's He Up To?
Law student at the
University Of Texas

Marital Status
Single

A Famous Name And Now, A Famous Face

The terms "superstar" and "politics" don't usually go together, but in the case of

"George P." greets attendees of the Puerto Rican Day Parade in New York City in June 2000.

George P. (the "P" is for "Prescott," the name of his great-grandfather, who was a U.S. senator from Connecticut), they do. Immediately after the Rice University graduate started stumping for his uncle's presidential campaign, he earned the title of George W.'s "secret weapon." His charisma mesmerized the public. Not only did he bring in the Hispanic and youth votes, he also began receiving the kind of attention usually reserved for A-list celebrities: at his every appearance, camera bulbs flashed, interviewers clamored to get his time and young women swooned. George P. became a media "catch" that boosted not only his uncle's ratings, but those of the programs who snared him on their screens.

It Wasn't Always This Way

Given this level of exposure, plus George P.'s apparent comfort in the face of it, you might think he's had years of similar experience. In reality, though, this was all quite new. True, his earliest childhood memory is of his 4-year-old self at a rally, wearing a "Bush for President" T-shirt and holding a balloon during his grandfather's unsuccessful 1980 campaign. But for the most part, his childhood was a very private one. Like his younger siblings, Noelle and Jeb Jr. (both of whom are, even now, virtually unknown to the world), George P. was raised strictly out of the limelight, protected as much as possible from public interference. His Mexican-born mother, Columba, made it her mission to rear bilingual children and to give them an appreciation for the Latin cul-

Sage Advice

In George Bush's memoirs, *All The Best, George Bush*, he includes this advice to George P. who was away at baseball camp: "May all your swings turn into line drives, and may all your pitches be over the plate; and if you get a bad bounce in life, shake it off and grab the next one."

Where He Stands

"P." is the oldest of George and Barbara Bush's 15 grandchildren. The next oldest is his sister, Noelle.

George P. Bush plays to the crowd before giving his speech at the 2000 Republican National Convention.

ture of her own roots. An exclusive prep school in Coral Gables, Florida, provided the rest of George P.'s education, and after graduation he headed off to Rice University in Houston and to a major in history.

College life was private for George P., as well. Rice was within visiting distance of his grandparents, George and Barbara Bush, with whom he is very close. He has laughingly referred to his grandmother as "the family enforcer," and credits his grandfather with teaching him table manners and "to be myself – not arrogant – and not show off." He ate many Sunday dinners with the elder Bushes and steered clear of most of the high-profile clubs during his time at Rice. He did join the baseball team in his freshman year, but got little playing time and quit by the time he was a sophomore. He also volunteered as a coach and mentor for urban youth, an experience that may have inspired the step he took after his 1998 graduation – accepting a job teaching history at a high school in a low-income community south of Miami.

George On Being A Bush

George P. has discussed the possible pitfalls, as well as the benefits, of being a member of the Bush clan. While recognizing that his name has been a sort of "passport" to experiencing extraordinary things, he has said, "At times I ask myself, 'Am I going to be able to live life the way I want to?' I'm cautious about doing certain things, but I'm definitely not complaining about my life, at all."

Livin' La Vida Loca

George P.'s public debut occurred quite suddenly. He had left the teaching profession and moved to Los Angeles to pursue a legal career. At the same time, his uncle's presidential campaign was heating up, and the younger George agreed to speak to area Latino groups on his uncle's behalf. Campaign aides were astounded by George P.'s public reception – everyone smiled and cheered and wanted to shake his hand. The young man was a natural spokesperson, switching easily from English to Spanish when answering reporters' questions, and generally charming everyone in sight. A star, as they say, was definitely born.

George P. Bush addresses the GOP Youth Caucus at the Republican National Convention.

Before long, George P. was filming television ads for the campaign, giving interviews to both major and minor media and traveling the country in support of his uncle. His popularity led the presidential candidate to joke that he and his brother Jeb had better stop using George P.'s campaign services, lest he steal all their press. For his part, George P.'s father expressed amusement over the fact that his boy was now called a hunk by the world at large. Barbara Bush rounded out the family's ribbing by telling George P. not to be "a showoff" and to keep his speeches short.

All teasing aside, the rest of the Bush clan seemed proud of their budding celebrity, and George W. took to introducing him as "a star in our family." George P. won the prestigious post of Youth Chairman for the National Republican Convention, and was among those chosen to introduce his uncle just moments before George W. accepted his party's nomination. But even as he labored in the political arena, George P. had his own future plans, and for now, he said repeatedly, they didn't involve his own run for public office. He'd been accepted for enrollment at the University of Texas School of Law and would soon become a student once more. He began his studies in the Fall 2000 term and if he finishes his coursework there, he will be the first in his family to become a lawyer.

Noelle
Bush
Niece
of the president

Full Name
Noelle Lucila Bush

Birth Date
July 1977

Birthplace
Houston

What's She Up To?
Recent graduate of Tallahassee Community College

Marital Status
Single

Jeb's Daughter

The second of Jeb and Columba's three children, Noelle Bush should be familiar to Bush supporters, as she made a name for herself at 1989's "Salute To The First Lady" party that was held in honor of her grandmother. Noelle stole the show when took the stage and played the accordion with a mariachi band that was performing at the event. Noelle Bush recently graduated from Tallahassee Community College.

Noelle Bush, shown here as a teen.

Jeb
Bush Jr.
Nephew
of the president

Full Name
John Ellis "Jeb" Bush Jr.

Birth Date
1983

Resides
Tallahassee, Florida

What's He Up To?
High school student

Jeb's Son

Jeb Bush Jr is known to the Bush clan as "Jebby." He's currently a high school student attending a prestigious prep school and therefore, Jeb Jr.'s been practically unheard from in the world of politics. Jeb Jr. did receive some unwanted media attention recently when local authorities found him in an compromising position with a young woman in a mall parking lot. But as he's still not out of his teens, Jeb Jr. will surely move on to more newsworthy achievements.

A young Jeb Bush Jr. posing for a family photo taken in 1991.

© Robert Maass/CORBIS

Neil
Bush

Brother
of the president

★ WHO IS NEIL BUSH ANYWAY? The third son of former President and First Lady George and Barbara Bush, he is the younger brother of Florida governor Jeb Bush and President George W. Bush. He is one of the more media-shy members of the Bush clan.

Full Name
Neil Mallon Bush

Birth Date
January 22, 1955

Birthplace
Midland, Texas

Resides
Houston

What's He Up To?
Director of Interlink, a communications consulting firm

Marital Status
Married to Sharon Bush

Children
Lauren, Pierce and Ashley

Unlike some of the other members of his famous family, Neil Bush relishes life outside of politics. Although at one time this Bush might have nursed political ambitions, for now he is content to raise his three school-aged children – Lauren, Pierce and Ashley – in his Houston home with Sharon, his wife of more than 20 years.

Hard Times

Neil's reluctance to seek the spotlight is understandable. He survived a bout of notoriety in the press in the late 1980s and early 1990s as a result of his association with the Denver-based Silverado Banking, Savings & Loan Association, which went bust in 1988. Neil sat on the board of the corporation and was accused (though never indicted) of having approved and profited from more than $100 million worth of questionable loans.

George Bush Presidential Library

Neil has always denied any wrongdoing, and felt at the time that he was being unfairly persecuted

Neil and Sharon Bush with their children, Pierce, Ashley and Lauren.

just because he was the (then) president's son. He said, "I've always prided myself on being the lowest-profile member of the Bush family, and suddenly this thing has exploded."

A low-profile was not exactly what he got when *PEOPLE* magazine named him one of its "25 Most Intriguing People Of 1990" as a result of the attention his situation drew. Through it all, his family supported him, including his mother, Barbara. During the ordeal, Neil said, "I think she worried about it more than I do. She hates it when people beat up on her kids."

The situation was finally resolved in 1992 when Neil agreed to pay $50,000 to settle civil litigation bought against him in relation to the savings and loan collapse.

A Second Camelot

Although many observers have compared the Bushes to the Kennedys, they have not seemed willing to embrace that likeness. During George W. Bush's 2000 presidential campaign, however, Neil said that he was willing to accept the comparison. "If what that means is dedication to public service, then we'll take it," he said.

Family Tree

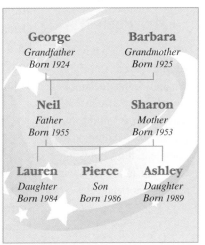

George
Grandfather
Born 1924

Barbara
Grandmother
Born 1925

Neil
Father
Born 1955

Sharon
Mother
Born 1953

Lauren
Daughter
Born 1984

Pierce
Son
Born 1986

Ashley
Daughter
Born 1989

Neil Bush – George W.'s Brother

Culture Shock

In 1966, 11-year-old Neil experienced his first taste of the changes his father's political career would bring when the family moved from Midland, Texas to Washington, D.C. He has said, "There I was with a heavy Texas accent, white socks and a crew cut. I had a terrible first half year. I got zapped into D.C. before I could enjoy any celebrity in Houston. In D.C. I was just another kid on the block. And my parents wouldn't let me get away with being swell-headed. No airs, no posing."

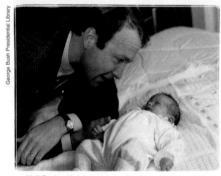

Neil Bush with his youngest daughter, Ashley, in 1989.

It was also about this time that, while attending posh St. Albans prep school in Washington, D.C., Neil was diagnosed with dyslexia. One of his teachers told Mrs. Bush that he might never graduate from high school due to his learning disability. In typical Bush fashion, however, Barbara Bush dismissed that prognosis and instead worked with him on a special remedial program to get him back on track. As a result, not only did he graduate from high school, but during his senior year he received a special award in recognition of his achievement.

Mr. Perfect

When Neil was a boy, his siblings used to affectionately refer to him as "Mr. Perfect" because he was the one child his parents could count on to complete his chores on time and abide by their sometimes strict rules.

Neil left D.C. after high school to attend Tulane University in New Orleans. He graduated with a bachelor's degree in international relations and went on to earn an M.B.A. from Tulane in 1979.

The Campaign Trail

A staunch supporter of his father, he worked on all of the elder Bush's national campaigns. It was while stumping for his father in New Hampshire during the 1980 presidential primaries that he met his wife-to-be, a pretty young schoolteacher named Sharon Smith. She didn't have much of an interest in politics, and that was fine with Neil. He has said, "Sharon really didn't care about those primaries, and to me it was nice

Neil Bush in an informal chat with Bush supporters at the 2000 Republican National Convention.

to have a nonpolitical girlfriend." After a short courtship, the two married and began their life together in Denver, determined, in Neil's words, "to be independent and not travel on anyone's coattails."

Following in his family's footsteps, his first business venture was an oil-exploration firm. The timing was not quite right and by 1985, he was ready to get out and accepted an invitation to join the Silverado board of directors.

Moving Toward The Future

Today, with the Silverado mess behind him, Neil and his family live in Houston. He is employed by Interlink Management Corporation, an international communications consulting firm, which is run out of the same building in which his father has an office.

He's Just A Friendly Guy

Mary Matalin, one of George H.W. Bush's top campaign advisors in both 1988 and 1992, described Neil in this fashion: "He likes people, and he's just perpetually chipper." He sounds like a fun guy to have around!

Neil has also carried on the Bush family's legacy of charitable work. Both he and Sharon are very active in Houston's social and business circles and, subsequently, they often find themselves on the guest list (and are sometimes even the hosts) of lavish fund-raising galas. Neil has also helped the Americares organization, which is one the largest non-profit disaster-relief organizations in the United States. Both Neil's mother and his uncle

(Prescott) serve on the organization's advisory committee.

For now, Neil is busy with a pet project – preparing an Internet-based educational reform program. His son Pierce was diagnosed with Attention Deficit Disorder (ADD), and the program, which is based in Austin and called Ignite!, is an outgrowth of the difficulties he and his family faced as a result of the diagnosis. The goal of the program, he says, is to "build an educational system that's adaptable to the child." One of his biggest concerns is the

Neil Bush enjoys the outdoors in this 1990 photo.

George Bush Presidential Library

prescribing of Ritalin for children diagnosed with ADD. He has said, "There are 6 to 8 million kids being put on mind-altering drugs, and 80% of them are boys. We need instead to arm out teachers with the right tools to engage each child so they don't tune out."

The amount of his time the project consumes is one reason that Neil gave for not being very visible during his elder brother's presidential campaign, although others have speculated that he is still wary of the media.

Making His Move

Neil recently told a group of Colorado Republicans that he and Sharon would be moving back to Colorado – but without their kids. They'll wait until the children are out of high school before they move out of Texas.

Although he has not been the most visible Bush, Neil has supported both Jeb and George W. in their political endeavors. He helped raise money for Jeb in Florida, and he appeared briefly on *Larry King Live* to show his support for George during the 2000 campaign. Does Neil feel any differently towards George W. now that he's president? Apparently not. "He's just my brother. I was raised with this guy," he has said.

Sharon
Bush

George Bush Presidential Library

Sister-In-Law
of the president

★ WHO IS SHARON BUSH ANYWAY? The spouse of Neil Bush, Sharon is a mother of three and founder of the Karitas Foundation, an organization devoted to raising funds to help children in need.

As a young schoolteacher living in New Hampshire, Sharon Smith probably never dreamed that one day she would become part of one of America's most powerful and influential political families. That's just what happened, however, when she was introduced to Neil Bush, the son of former president George Bush, when he was campaigning for his father in New Hampshire during the 1980 presidential campaign.

Sharing Her Good Fortune

After a whirlwind courtship, Neil and Sharon were married and the two moved to Denver, Colorado, in 1981. Although she gave up teaching, her compassion and desire to help children only grew stronger with the passing years.

Full Name
Sharon Smith Bush

Birth Date
1953

Resides
Houston

What's She Up To?
Founder of Karitas, which raises funds for children's charities

Marital Status
Married to Neil Bush

Children
Lauren, Pierce and Ashley

In Denver, she volunteered at Children's Hospital and went on to work for other charitable causes. Then, in 1989, Sharon founded the Karitas Foundation, which is dedicated to raising funds for charities devoted to helping children. She has said that she came up with the idea for Karitas during the 1988 presidential election. Sharon was quoted as saying, "At the time, there was a lot of media interest in what the presidential candidates' families were doing. I decided to turn that attention around to focus on a new children's charity." Sharon's charitable instincts come naturally to her. She has said, "Life is so short. You're lucky if you're in a position to give back. It's such a good feeling."

Charity Begins At Home

In 1991, when Sharon, her husband and their three children moved from Denver to Houston, she continued her work with Karitas. By then, her oldest child, Lauren, was 7, and Sharon was already making sure that her children understood the importance of giving back to the community. In a 1991 interview she said, "My own children understand that they are very fortunate, and that we need to help those who are less fortunate. Karitas is a good learning experience for them."

Her mother-in-law, Barbara Bush, who herself is an avid campaigner for literacy, said in 1989 of Sharon and Karitas, "I'm really proud of Sharon. I think it's just incredible she's taken the initiative to get involved in this new and wonderful project."

Something Old, Something New...

Sharon and Neil were married in St. Ann's Church in Kennebunkport, Maine – the same church that Neil's grandparents, Prescott and Dorothy Bush, were married in more than 60 years earlier.

A Woman Of Distinction

In the Houston community where the family lives, Sharon is known for being incredibly civic-minded and generous. Since arriving at the city, she has helped develop the Houston Healthy Families program through a start-up grant that was given by the Karitas Foundation. For a time, she served on the Board of Directors of the Child Abuse Prevention Network, and she is currently a board member of the Houston Dress For Success program, which is a non-profit organization that is devoted to dressing underprivileged women for the workplace.

Additionally, Sharon's name frequently appears in the society columns as an attendee of several different Houston-area charity events. She and Neil are very respected and well-liked in their community. In fact, Sharon was recently honored for all of her hard work and dedication to charitable organizations. She was named a Woman of Distinction in January 2001 at Houston's Winter Ball.

Barbara Bush (third from left) spends some quality time with daughter-in-law Sharon Bush (left) and her grandchildren just before George Bush's inauguration in 1989.

Super Mom

Sharon is also an important force in her children's lives, making sure that their family and studies come first. Her daughter Lauren, is now a part-time model and Sharon often accompanies her to fashion shoots. *W* magazine, which did a photo shoot with Lauren, reported that Sharon wouldn't let her daughter undress with male hair dressers and other male professionals around, as other models often do.

Sharon's grace and aplomb in handling social situations seem to have been passed along to her children, and will surely serve them well as the next generation of Bushes to enter the public eye.

© Tim Griffith/Camera Press/Retna LTD

Lauren
Bush

Niece
of the president

★ **WHO IS LAUREN BUSH ANYWAY?** The president's niece, Lauren is also a part-time model who has appeared in several fashion magazines. She is the daughter of Neil and Sharon Bush and lives in Houston, Texas, where she attends a private high school.

Full Name
Lauren Pierce Bush

Birth Date
June 26, 1984

Birthplace
Denver

Resides
Houston

What's She Up To?
Part-time model
and full-time high
school student

Though she may come from one of America's most famous political dynasties, Lauren Bush is attracting fame for something else entirely – making quite a name for herself in the modeling industry. Of course, she still has to finish high school first.

No Stranger To The Spotlight

Having grown up as a member of the Bush clan, Lauren is no stranger to the spotlight. She was 4 years old when her grandfather, George Bush, was elected president in 1988 and she remembers her grandfather's years in the White House fondly, saying, "I can remember sliding down banisters in the White House when I was a kid;

Reminiscent Of Another Political Family

Bruce Weber, who photographed Lauren for Abercrombie & Fitch, said of her, "She's pretty enough to be a Kennedy."

© Tim Griffiths/Camera Press/Retna LTD

Lauren Bush, daughter of Neil Bush, began modeling when she was only 13.

rolling up carpets with my 14 cousins and generally going on the rampage . . . we even used to race in and out of the tours . . . it used to make Grandma mad."

It seems Lauren adjusted to fame at an early age. When her grandfather left office and returned to Houston in 1993, 8-year-old Lauren was waiting for her grandparents with an armful of flowers at their Houston home. She was asked for comment by a reporter and replied, "To tell you the truth, I thought it would be much 'crowdeder.' I'm glad because now I can walk around."

Smile For The Camera

Lauren first started modeling when she was 13 years old, and has since signed a contract with the New York–based Elite modeling agency. Her picture has graced such magazines as *Vogue, W* and *George,* and she's appeared in advertisements for the popular clothing company Abercrombie & Fitch. Her booker at Elite describes her as "a classic beauty, with an athletic build." But modeling is just a part-time endeavor for Lauren and is confined to weekends and school vacations. Her full-time efforts are concentrated on her schoolwork.

She Knows What She Wants

Lauren may have inherited some of grandmother Barbara Bush's strength and resolve. The vegetarian and animal rights activist has said, "I have strong beliefs and my family appreciates that."

Belle Of The Ball

In 2000, Lauren participated in the Crillon Haute Couture Ball held in Paris, an event in which young debutantes from all over the globe "come out" to society. And it's not just a society event – the ball doubles as a fund-raiser for AIDS and cancer research.

Lauren wore a Christian Dior dress and was escorted by French Prince Louis de Bourbon. A family friend who attended the event said, "Lauren was the star of the whole evening. She was like a princess." Her parents, Neil and Sharon Bush, were aglow as well. Sharon reportedly said, "It was a true Cinderella evening. It was beyond our expectations." Although Neil was no doubt just as excited, he said, "We haven't dared tell her grandmother she is taking time off [from school] to come here. She wouldn't approve."

Lauren strikes a pose while on a modeling assignment.

A Royal Crush

The tabloids have recently reported that Lauren has been involved in an e-mail "romance" with Prince William. It seems that the two teenagers have never met but first became acquainted when Lauren sent the prince one of her modeling photos. Intrigued, the prince responded by sending her a photograph of himself. The two exchanged e-mail addresses and have been corresponding for the last couple of years. "Wills," as the prince is called, has been described as the "most eligible bachelor in the world."

Just A Typical Teenager

Despite the fairy tale aspects of her life, Lauren insists she is a typical teenager. She says, "I like what I'm doing. I mean, I'm just having fun." Sounds like she's got her head on straight and her priorities in order.

A Terrific Texan

In 1999, Lauren was picked by *Texas Monthly* magazine as one of their "Texas Twenty." Such recognition means that Lauren is one of the "most impressive, intriguing and influential Texans in 1999."

Pierce
Bush

Nephew
of the president

AP/WWP

★ WHO IS PIERCE BUSH ANYWAY? Pierce made quite an impression at the 2000 Republican National Convention, where the outgoing youngster campaigned for his uncle and was interviewed by CNN and Larry King.

It seems that Neil Bush can relate to his son, Pierce. Both are middle children and both have been diagnosed with learning disabilities – Neil with dyslexia and Pierce with Attention Deficit Disorder. However, unlike his dad, who tends to shun the spotlight, Pierce seems to enjoy life in the public eye. Having attended two previous political conventions, the well-spoken Houston high schooler made a name for himself at the 2000 Republican National Convention with his quick wit and easygoing style.

Says his uncle, Florida governor Jeb Bush, "Pierce is the kind of guy that would get on the floor . . . when the Rockettes [dancers for the Houston Rockets basketball team] . . . would get out and dance, and get out and dance with them. So he's kind

Full Name
Pierce Mallon Bush

Birth Date
March 15, 1986

Birthplace
Denver

Resides
Houston

What's He Up To?
High school student

65

of an extrovert." A reporter from the *Seattle Times,* who encountered Pierce when he was making his way through the 2000 convention, said of the George W.'s nephew, "He's almost frighteningly precocious and at ease."

A young Pierce Bush toddles to retrieve his stuffed monkey during a family photo in January 1989.

Tough Times

Pierce, who at one point attended an all-boys boarding school in the East (he's now enrolled in high school in Houston), has struggled with some of the same issues as his father, Neil, who had a difficult time in school until he was diagnosed with dyslexia. In an interview with Larry King, Neil said of Pierce, "He's an incredibly talented young kid . . . . Pierce has been in this school where, despite the fact that he's truly gifted, he had a lot of difficulty in 6th, 7th and 8th grade. And he was diagnosed by some as ADD. They tried to put him on Ritalin. Pierce refused to take Ritalin. And so we took him to a place where they did a full assessment . . . and came to the conclusion that Pierce is a gifted and talented kid." Neil's experience with Pierce led him to begin creating educational software designed to appeal to kids who have a difficult time with more traditional teaching techniques.

Grandma Knows Best

When asked by Larry King about his famous grandmother, the former first lady, Pierce said, "She always makes me do my summer reading." That's what happens when your grandmother is the Honorary Chairman of the Barbara Bush Foundation for Family Literacy!

Looking To The Future

At the Republican National Convention, it was clear Pierce holds his uncle George W. Bush in high regard, telling a CNN reporter that, "[George W. Bush] is going to restore dignity to the office . . . which has not been the case for the last eight or seven years." Pierce, who says politics "runs in the family," doesn't talk much about politics with Uncle George, however. Instead, they talk baseball. "He's a big Rangers fan. I live in Houston, so I'm an Astros fan," explains Pierce.

At the age of 14, Pierce found himself in the spotlight campaigning for Uncle George at the 2000 Republican National Convention in August.

Pierce claims he will call his uncle "Prez." Some have wondered if Pierce himself will someday be known by the same moniker, considering his early interest in politics, as well as his camera-savvy personality. Only time will tell. But Pierce, who at his young age has already attended three Republican National Conventions and impressed reporters and family alike, has already proven that politics is truly in his blood.

Ashley
Bush

Niece
of the president

Full Name
Ashley Walker Bush

Birth Date
February 7, 1989

Birthplace
Denver

Resides
Houston

What's She Up To?
Elementary school
student

Neil's Daughter

Like her siblings, Ashley was born in Denver and raised in Houston. She was born on February 7, 1989 and baptized on Easter Sunday, the first Easter her grandparents spent in the White House. Unlike her sister, who is a model, Ashley has managed to stay out of the public eye, yet she does make a public appearance now and again. Ashley attends school in Houston and can be seen attending charity events with her parents, Neil and Sharon.

Ashley is the youngest child of Neil and Sharon Bush.

Marvin
Bush

Brother
of the president

★ WHO IS MARVIN BUSH ANYWAY? The youngest son of George and Barbara Bush, Marvin has come into his own through managing a successful investment business and beating a disease that nearly took his life.

Full Name
Marvin Pierce Bush

Birth Date
October 22, 1956

Birthplace
Midland, Texas

Resides
Alexandria, Virginia

What's He Up To?
Investment executive

Marital Status
Married to Margaret Bush

Children
Marshall and Walker

While his brothers have followed their father's footsteps into politics, businessman Marvin Bush has emphatically resisted a political life. "I think it's unusual that my brothers – or anybody else for that matter – would ever want to get into politics," he told one reporter. The youngest son of George and Barbara has, for the most part, avoided the limelight, believing that the desire for politics is born in your system, not bred.

Last, But Not Least

Born on October 22, 1956, in Midland Texas, Marvin Pierce Bush was given the name of his mother's father, Marvin Pierce, a president of the McCall Corporation who was known for his sharp wit. Growing up,

Marvin had three older brothers to emulate. Being the youngest boy, Marvin often found himself in George W., Jeb or Neil's shadow, but he soon learned that he didn't have to compete with his siblings. Marvin struck out on his own path in life, realizing that he didn't have to prove anything to anyone but himself.

Margaret and Marvin Bush enjoy family time with their kids Walker (left) and Marshall (right) in September 1991.

From Coast To Coast

When his father was elected to Congress in 1966, the family moved from Texas to Washington. Marvin was enrolled at the Woodberry Forest boarding school in Charlottesville, Virginia.

Always an excellent athlete, Marvin was a member of the Woodberry basketball team when he found himself up against a player for the opposing team, St. Christopher's, named Scott Andrews. The two were re-acquainted when they both attended the University of Virginia and the young men struck up a friendship that would later lead to a life-changing business venture.

Marvin's relationship with Scott was not the only one that he made at the University of Virginia that would stand the test of time. It was there that Marvin met Margaret Molster, who became his bride upon his graduation in 1981. The two went on to start a family, adopting daughter Marshall in 1986 and son Walker in 1989.

Eschewing political life after school, Marvin went on to work at a string of financial corporations,

Family Tree

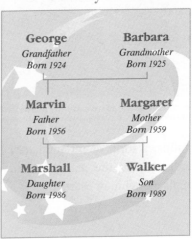

George	Barbara
Grandfather	*Grandmother*
Born 1924	*Born 1925*

Marvin	Margaret
Father	*Mother*
Born 1956	*Born 1959*

Marshall	Walker
Daughter	*Son*
Born 1986	*Born 1989*

What's In A Name?

Marvin's middle name, which is his mother's maiden name, comes from Franklin Pierce, a former president and a great, great, great uncle of Barbara Bush's father.

learning everything there possibly was to know about the business of venture capitalism.

A Health Scare Takes Its Toll

However, while Marvin should have been enjoying his success in business and his life as the vice president's son, a sudden illness began to slow him down. He found himself in constant stomach pain, he lost a great amount of weight and he often had to fight the urge to use the bathroom up to 20 times a day. Marvin discovered he had a serious case of ulcerative

Marvin Bush (center) and his sister, Doro (left) and brother, Neil (right), talk with Larry King about Bush family life and George W.'s campaign, while seated above the Republican National Convention on August 3, 2000.

colitis, a form of inflammatory bowel disease. He had to undergo surgery, and the damaged part of his intestine was removed and replaced with an ostomy.

School Days

Marvin attended the University of Texas for one year before transferring to the University of Virginia, from which he graduated in 1981.

A Stroke Of Luck

After his recovery, Marvin received a tip from a friend in the investment business. A privately-held waste management company was looking for investors and Marvin had the opportunity to get in on it. He called his old friend Scott Andrews and the two decided to invest, as partners, in the business. The risk paid off and the two made a hefty profit.

In 1993, Marvin and Scott joined together with another friend, Bill Trimble, to co-found Winston Partners Group. Named after Winston Churchill, the Alexandria, Virginia-based $300 million investment brokerage firm focuses on hedge fund and private equity investments.

Marvin (top row, second from right) and friends and family of George W. Bush celebrate his nomination at the Republican National Convention. First row, from left: Lois and Roland Betts (George's friend from Yale), Laura and George W. Bush. Second row, from left: Dorothy Bush Koch, Walker Bush and his parents, Margaret and Marvin, and Jenna Welch, Laura's mom.

The Family Speaks Out

How has his family reacted to his lack of interest in politics? "I'm not surprised he's forged a path in the investment world," Barbara Bush told reporters, "He's always been very centered, very bright. Besides, he's always hated politics. We could never get him to come to the White House."

Marvin is not the first Bush family member to choose finance over politics as a career. Prescott Bush, Marvin's late grandfather, spent many of his years as a partner at the Wall Street firm of Brown

Brothers Harriman & Co. before serving as a U.S. senator. Also, two of Marvin's uncles, Jonathan and William, opened their own successful financial advisory businesses. And, Marvin's brother Neil has also dallied in the financial world.

AP/WWP

Marvin and his mother, Barbara Bush, share the excitement of the convention in August, 2000.

Using The Public Eye For The Good Of Others

In his spare time, Marvin continues to promote awareness of the disease that nearly took his life. He has served as a spokesman for the Crohn's & Colitis Foundation of America and has been a major contributor to the United Ostomy Association. Marvin says that the surgery has eased his pain, and improved his life tremendously. He now lives a normal life, free of discomfort.

Talking about his disease is the one public part of his life. Marvin has spent many hours counseling individuals by phone, presenting public service ads, and appearing on talk shows to discuss the sensitive details of his disease. Though it is not the most comfortable subject, Marvin believes that if he can make a difference in anyone's life who is ill, he believes that he has done his job.

Between running his successful investment firm and helping those who suffer from colitis, Marvin is secure in his success, both as a businessman and as a family man.

Family Comes First

Although Marvin generally tries to avoid the spotlight surrounding his family, he played an active role in helping both his father and his brother campaign for president.

Margaret
Bush

George Bush Presidential Library

Sister-In-Law
of the president

★ WHO IS MARGARET BUSH ANYWAY? She's the wife of Marvin Bush and the mother of their two children, Marshall and Walker. Margaret is a gentle woman with great inner strength which has helped her overcome life's misfortunes.

In the summer of 1981, many watched the famous royal wedding of Prince Charles and Lady Diana and marveled at its pomp and circumstance. That same summer, Marvin Bush married his college sweetheart, Margaret Molster, in a ceremony that, according to Barbara Bush, "looked like much more fun."

Ups And Downs

Margaret was raised in Richmond, Virginia by a large and loving family. She first met Marvin Bush at the University of Virginia – her older brother, Chip, was Marvin's roommate – and the two eventually fell in love.

The couple settled in Virginia and enjoyed a happy life together until Marvin

Full Name
Margaret Molster Bush

Birth Date
March 1959

Birthplace
Richmond, Virginia

Resides
Alexandria, Virginia

What's She Up To?
Full-time mom
and aspiring actress

Marital Status
Married to Marvin Bush

Children
Marshall and Walker

was diagnosed with colitis at the age of 29. Margaret stood by his side and was a tremendous support to her husband and the entire Bush family throughout Marvin's illness. Margaret knew how to be strong in the face of a medical emergency,

Margaret Bush presents her daughter, Marshall, with a birthday cake during a family celebration in 1991.

since she is a cancer survivor. When she was just 6 years old, she was diagnosed with ovarian cancer, a practically unheard of medical condition in such a young girl. With surgery and radiation, Margaret made a full recovery.

Marvin's bout with colitis brought the couple closer together and they decided to start a family. The loving couple was forced to adopt, because Margaret's cancer treatments left her unable to bear her own children. Margaret and Marvin worked with a private, non-profit adoption agency in Fort Worth, Texas, and received their first child, daughter Marshall, in 1986. Three years later, working through the same agency,   they adopted Walker.

Taking To The Stage and Screen

Now that her children are in school, Margaret, a former teacher, has focused her attention on another goal – acting. She has taken classes at the New York School for Film and Television, but tries to accept as much work as she can in the Washington D.C. area. "I am a mother first and foremost, and studying or working here allows me to be with my children," she told one reporter.

With two health scares behind her, a loving family to support her and a budding acting career in the works, Margaret Bush has much to be thankful for.

Marshall
Bush
Niece
of the president

Full Name
Marshall Lloyd Bush

Birth Date
June 1986

Birthplace
Ft. Worth, Texas

Resides
Alexandria, Virginia

What's She Up To?
High school student

Marvin's Daughter

In June of 1986, Marvin and Margaret Bush adopted their first child – a baby girl whom they named Marshall Lloyd Bush – from the Edna Gladney Home in Fort Worth, Texas. Marshall made headlines in 1991 when, as a tot, she was rescued from the White House

Marshall Bush is the oldest daughter of Marvin and Margaret Bush.

swimming pool where a family dog had been holding her underwater. Marshall is the owner of Ranger, one of former "first dog" Millie's pups and a brother of current first dog, Spot.

Walker
Bush
Nephew
of the president

Full Name
Charles Walker Bush

Birth Date
November, 1989

Birthplace
Ft. Worth, Texas

Resides
Alexandria, Virginia

What's He Up To?
Elementary school student

Marvin's Son

Marvin and Margaret's second child, Charles Walker Bush, was born in November of 1989, and adopted by the couple shortly thereafter. Known simply as "Walker" by his friends and family, he is adored and loved by the entire Bush clan. Young Walker captivated the country when he helped his

Walker looks purely professional at the 2000 Republican National Convention.

grandmother, Barbara, place the star on the National Christmas Tree in 1991, which was George and Barbara's last year in the White House.

Dorothy Bush Koch

Sister
of the president

★ WHO IS DOROTHY BUSH KOCH ANYWAY? The youngest child of George and Barbara, this mother of four tends to stay out of the spotlight unless one of her family members is running for office. Then she's ready to hop on the campaign trail by raising money and making public appearances.

Full Name
Dorothy Walker
Bush Koch

Birth Date
August 18, 1959

Birthplace
Midland, Texas

Resides
Bethesda, Maryland

What's She Up To?
Fundraiser for
several charities

Marital Status
Married to Bobby Koch

Children
Sam and Ellie LeBlond,
Robert and Gigi Koch

It is almost surprising that Dorothy Bush Koch never went into politics herself. After all, her family has a long tradition of civic leaders, including her father, who was vice president and president and, of course, her eldest brother, who is following in his father's footsteps as president. But Dorothy is happy doing her own thing. Her charity and volunteer work, as well as her husband and four children, keep her busy. And although she is part of the "Bush dynasty," there's more to Dorothy than just her family ties.

It's A Girl!

Dorothy was born on August 18, 1959 as Dorothy Walker Bush – named after her grandmother – although her family quickly

Christening In China

On her 16th birthday in 1975, Doro was christened at a church in Beijing, China. Her brother Marvin was a stand-in for her godparents.

George Bush Presidential Library

Doro and her father, George Bush, share a moment in December 1990.

began calling her Doro. Like most of her siblings, she was born in Texas. She is the Bush family's only surviving daughter. Another girl, Robin, had died six years earlier from leukemia at the age of 3 .

Doro's schooling included attending the United Nations school and eventually boarding school. It was at this time, in 1974, that her parents moved to China so her father could serve as a diplomat. She and her brothers would visit during their summer breaks from school. Doro then went on to attend Boston College and graduated in 1982. That September, she married Bill LeBlond, a building contractor, in Kennebunkport, Maine. The newlyweds remained in Maine where Doro worked for the state's Office of Tourism. In 1984, they had their first child, a boy, Sam, who was followed in 1986 by a little girl, Ellie.

Unfortunately, the marriage was not meant to last. In 1990, she was officially divorced from Bill and moved with her two children to Washington, D.C., to be closer to her parents and to work at a new job with the National Rehabilitation Hospital. She worked in the Communications

Family Tree

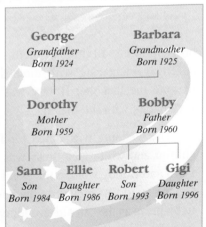

George	Barbara
Grandfather	*Grandmother*
Born 1924	*Born 1925*

Dorothy	Bobby
Mother	*Father*
Born 1959	*Born 1960*

Sam	Ellie	Robert	Gigi
Son	*Daughter*	*Son*	*Daughter*
Born 1984	*Born 1986*	*Born 1993*	*Born 1996*

and Development Office and by all accounts loved her work. By now her father was president, and being the nation's "first daughter" meant that her divorce was anything but private knowledge.

Love Is In The Air

Life went on and Doro began to date again – although it was not an easy task for a divorced woman with two children, who also happened to be the president's daughter! She had been seriously dating Bobby Koch (pronounced "cook") – gasp! a democrat! – for some time and by 1992, Bobby was ready to take the next step.

George Bush Presidential Library

While Doro was heading the U.S. delegation to the Winter Olympics in Albertville, France, Bobby met with her father at presidential retreat Camp David to declare his intention to marry Doro. When Doro returned from France she received a wonderful Valentine's Day gift – a marriage proposal! Bobby took her and both of her children out to dinner where he made

Family resemblance? Dorothy Bush looks adoringly at her mother during an event held the week of George Bush's inauguration.

his proposal to all three of them. They all agreed and Doro received an engagement ring with three diamonds – one for each of them. Despite the fact that Bobby was a Democrat, Doro's parents were very happy with the match.

The wedding was slated for June 27th, 1992, and Doro's peach chiffon and white lace dress was designed by Arnold Scaasi. Both Doro and Bobby wanted the event to be a small, private ceremony, so Camp David was picked as the best location. The event was referred to by press as the "stealth wedding," as it was impossible to get information about the it beforehand. The rehearsal dinner, the night

Family Fashion Favorite

Arnold Scaasi, the designer of Doro's wedding dress, also designed Barbara Bush's mother-of-the-bride dress and Barbara's 1989 inauguration gown

before, was held in the White House's State Dining Room with about 70 people present. Doro, Sam and Ellie had written a special toast for Bobby in the form of a rap song.

The next day, in a chapel filled with peach roses, Doro and Bobby said their vows in front of just more than 100 guests. Both Sam and Ellie were in the wedding party along with Bobby's brothers. Everyone agreed it was a perfect day.

Doro, Bobby, Sam and Ellie currently reside in Bethesda, Maryland, with Doro and Bobby's new additions to the family, Robert and Gigi. Doro has continued her work with the National Rehabilitation Hospital on a volunteer basis and serves on the board of directors. Fundraising is her forte and she does it both for local charities and for family members' campaigns.

Duty Calls

Doro is certainly proud of the political members of her family and chips in whenever she can. Mary Matalin, key adviser for two of George Bush's presidential campaigns, spoke of Doro in the Dallas News, "She's no showboat. She doesn't seek out the microphone, but she doesn't shrivel from it, either."

Her first campaign efforts were in the late 1970s while she was attending

Reuters NewMedia Inc./CORBIS

George W. Bush and his sister, Dorothy talk to the crowd while traveling the campaign trail in 2000.

Boston College. Her father was campaigning for president and Doro wanted to help out. To prove her dedication she enrolled in a nine-month course at the Katherine Gibbs secretarial school, missing the family's summer vacation in Kennebunkport, Maine. She then put these new skills to work at the "Bush For President" headquarters in Boston.

Doro helped her father again during his subsequent presidential campaigns in 1988 and 1992. His defeat in 1992 was a severe disap-

George Bush Presidential Library

Dorothy and Ellie LeBlond spend some time with Barbara Bush in 1989.

pointment, but Doro's eldest brother George W. would later make up for it. When George W. decided to run for president in 2000, Doro was behind him 100%. She even became one of his fundraising "pioneers," pledging to raise $100,000 in $1,000 checks. She exceeded everyone's expectations and is credited with raising more money than any of George W.'s other so-called pioneers.

Doro may not be a politician herself, but there's no doubt that politics runs in her blood. You can be sure that the next time a Bush family member hits the campaign trail, Doro will be right behind him or her. And she will continue to make her own mark with her volunteer work and fundraising efforts.

Bobby
Koch

Brother-In-Law
of the president

George Bush Presidential Library

★ WHO IS BOBBY KOCH ANYWAY? This staunch Democrat is now part of a famous Republican family. He hasn't given up his political orientation, but he has switched to a non-partisan job as a lobbyist with the Wine Institute.

Though Bobby Koch married into a very political family, he had already made a name for himself in the political arena. He followed in the footsteps of his father, George Koch, who was a famous Washington lobbyist.

After graduating from the University of Maryland in 1983, Bobby went to work for the Democratic Congressional Campaign Committee which was chaired by Tony Coelho. Bobby worked his way up and eventually helped to make Coelho the House Majority Whip. When Coelho left Congress in 1989, Bobby was recruited by House Majority Leader Richard Gephardt and eventually became Gephardt's second-ranked staff member as his administrative assistant. Bobby was quickly climbing the political ladder.

Full Name
Robert P. Koch

Birth Date
1960

Birthplace
Washington, D.C.

Resides
Bethesda, Maryland

What's He Up To?
Washington, D.C. lobbyist

Marital Status
Married to
Dorothy Bush Koch

Children
Robert and Gigi Koch,
Sam and Ellie LeBlond
(stepchildren)

However, his life changed dramatically in 1992 when he left his job with Gephardt to become senior vice president and lobbyist for the Wine Institute.

That year, he also married the president's daughter, Doro, and became a family

Bobby and Doro at the 2000 GOP Convention.

man. Doro had two children from her previous marriage, Sam and Ellie, and the couple soon had two more of their own. Robert was born in 1993 and Gigi followed in 1996.

It surely wasn't easy being accepted as a Democrat in the Bush family but Doro's relatives were very excited about the match. Bobby has reciprocated by loyally supporting the Bushes in their political endeavors, and George W.'s campaign for president was treated no differently. Bobby worked with Doro in raising funds for her brother and he has publically declared that his vote was cast for George W.

Political Pranksters

When Bobby knelt with Doro at the altar for their June 1992 wedding everyone had a good laugh. Some jokesters, possibly his brothers, had put a Bush/Quayle sticker on the sole of his shoe.

Bobby's acceptance into the family certainly wasn't hurt by his enjoyment of one of father-in-law George Bush's favorite pastimes – golf.

Bobby lives with his wife and kids in Bethesda, Maryland, and continues to work for the Wine Institute. And just to prove that he hasn't totally changed political sides, he hosted a wine-tasting party for a Democratic representative in August 2000, just before the Democratic National Convention.

Sam
LeBlond
Nephew
of the president

Full Name
Samuel Bush
LeBlond

Birth Date
August 1984

Birthplace
Maine

Resides
Bethesda, Maryland

What's He Up To?
High school student

Dorothy's Son

Sam was born in 1984 when his grandfather was vice president and his mom, Doro, was married to Billy LeBlond. He lived in New England for much of his childhood, and then moved to Washington, D.C., in the early 1990s when his parents divorced. When his now-stepfather proposed to his mother in 1992, Bobby didn't ask only Doro to marry him, but asked Sam and his sister, Ellie, as well. Bush family lore says that Sam's reaction was an enthusiastic "Oh, yeah!"

Sam, shown here at 7 years old, is now a high school student.

Ellie
LeBlond
Niece
of the president

Full Name
Nancy Ellis LeBlond

Birth Date
January 19, 1986

Birthplace
Maine

Resides
Bethesda, Maryland

What's She Up To?
High school student

Dorothy's Daughter

George has described Ellie as "a beautiful girl – big eyes." Barbara, however, enjoys telling a story about a feistier girl. One day at school, Ellie was being taunted by a classmate because her grandfather had failed to win the U.S presidency in 1992. Ellie was doing a painting project at the time, and in retaliation to the taunts, she took her paintbrush, dipped it in red paint and swiped a thick red stripe down the other student's face and clothing!

George Bush clowning around with granddaughter Ellie at the 2000 Republican National Convention.

Dorothy's Son

Robert
Koch
Nephew
of the president

Robert Patrick Koch was the first child born to the marriage of Bobby and Doro Koch. Born on May 20, 1993, Robert's birth brought joy back into the Bush family, which had been saddened by the recent passing of Barbara Bush's older brother Jim.

While the Bush family will certainly support young Robert's future endeavors, they probably hope he doesn't follow exactly in his Democratic father's footsteps. Bobby has worked for some Democratic congressional stalwarts, including congressman Dick Gephardt. Robert, who is still in elementary school, currently resides in Bethesda, Maryland, with his family.

Full Name
Robert Patrick Koch

Birth Date
May 20, 1993

Birthplace
Washington, D.C.

Resides
Bethesda, Maryland

What's He Up To?
Elementary school student

Dorothy's Daughter

Gigi
Koch
Niece
of the president

Gigi Koch, whose full name is Georgia Grace Koch, was born on November 11, 1996. She is the newest addition to the Bush-Koch household, and the youngest of George and Barbara Bush's grandchildren.

Although Gigi is way too young to actively seek a role in politics, she can expect to find herself in the counsel of former president George Bush. Her grandpa plans to follow a family tradition by taking her on his fishing boat, where, when he's not teaching her how to cast her fishing rod to catch a snapping mackerel, he can share with her his grandfatherly wisdom.

Full Name
Georgia Grace Koch

Birth Date
November 11, 1996

Birthplace
Washington, D.C.

Resides
Bethesda, Maryland

What's She Up To?
Preschooler

Samuel Prescott Bush

Great-Grandfather
of the president

★ WHO IS SAMUEL BUSH ANYWAY? He's the great-grandfather of George W. Bush whose many contributions to society laid the foundation for the entire Bush family's political legacy.

E ven before his son became a U.S. senator, and his grandson and great-grandson became the 41st and 43rd presidents of the United States, Samuel Prescott Bush (who was called "S.P." by those who knew him) exemplified the industrious, patriotic spirit that would come to define the Bush family.

He's Been Working On the Railroad

Samuel was born in Brick Church, New Jersey, in 1863 to an Episcopal minister and

Family Tree

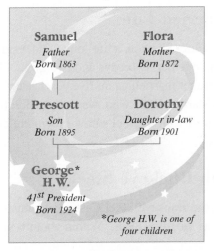

Samuel	Flora
Father	*Mother*
Born 1863	*Born 1872*

Prescott	Dorothy
Son	*Daughter in-law*
Born 1895	*Born 1901*

George* H.W.
41st President
Born 1924

*George H.W. is one of four children

Full Name
Samuel Prescott Bush

Birth Date
October 4, 1863

Death Date
February 8, 1948

Birthplace
Brick Church, New Jersey

What He's Best Known For
President of the Buckeye Steel Castings Company

Marital Status
Married to Flora Sheldon Bush

Children
Two girls and two boys, including George W.'s grandfather, Prescott

AP/WWP

A steam engine from the late 19th century – the era when Samuel P. Bush was earning his fortune working for a railroad company.

his wife. He spent his childhood in New York City where he attended public schools. He then went on to the Stevens Institute of Technology in Hoboken, New Jersey, where he graduated with a mechanical engineering degree in 1884.

After graduation he moved west and began working for the Pittsburgh, Cincinnati, Chicago, & St. Louis Railroad in Logansport, Indiana. He began as an apprentice and moved his way up, eventually relocating with the company to Columbus, Ohio, in 1885. Although Samuel ended up working for several different railroad companies, Columbus was the town where he would put down his roots and spend the rest of his life.

Married Life

In 1894, Samuel married Flora Sheldon, a life-long Ohio resident. The couple had four children together, two boys and two girls. Flora passed away in 1920, and Samuel married again five years later. His new wife was the former Martha Bell, who was originally from Milwaukee. She got along well with Samuel's now-grown children, who called her "Miss Martha."

Life With Buckeye Steel

In 1901, Samuel joined the Buckeye Steel Castings Company, a maker of railroad car parts, as vice-president. Within about 6 years,

A Snapshot Of The Past

Samuel Bush was an imposing man who stood more than six feet tall and had a powerful voice.

he had worked his way up to president. Buckeye, under Samuel's leadership, offered benefits for its employees that few companies of that time provided. The company started offering life insurance for its employees in 1917, bought land near the company for employee housing and began sponsoring educational and recreational activities for employees.

Samuel believed that the workplace should be a harmonious society in which employer and employee worked together for the same goal. Providing innovative benefits for his employees was a start toward reaching that goal.

While he might have been a compassionate employer, Samuel was by no means a pushover. As one colleague remembered him, he was "a snorter . . . Everyone knew when he was around; when he issued orders, boy it went!"

Though several other employers, including the Pennsylvania Railroad, tried to steal Samuel away from the company, he could never be persuaded to leave.

Samuel The Sportsman

Samuel Bush was quite a sportsman in his day. He was active in the YMCA's Businessman's Gym, and it has been said that he was responsible for starting up the first baseball league in Columbus, as well as its first tennis club.

A Humanitarian And A Leader

By most accounts, Samuel Bush was a well-rounded person. He was a sharp, hard-working businessman, but also one who was dedicated to social causes and deeply involved in community affairs. He was a man destined to leave his mark on history.

Samuel was elected mayor of his Columbus suburb of Marble Cliff and maintained that post for nearly all of the 1920s. But that wasn't the only thing Samuel was in charge of. He was the head of his local country club for a time, and was a director at the Federal Reserve Bank in Cleveland.

Within his profession, Samuel was a leader as well. He led the National Association for Manufacturers and the Ohio Manufacturer's Association. With the Ohio Manufacturer's Association, he was well known for his part in the association's fight for workmen's compensation laws – which isn't a surprising cause at all for such a diligent promoter of beneficial working conditions.

S.P. worked on a committee to battle Depression-era problems. Here, jobless men wait for food.

Merry Christmas!

S.P. is often described as enjoying his work and his position in life, and is also credited with having a dry sense of humor. In 1918, he wrote to Flora while she was visiting relatives. Discussing his Christmas present to her, he asked, "What do you think it is? Well, you can guess. A collar with a heavy chain to keep you at home."

Samuel's talents weren't just held to the environs of Columbus, Ohio, however. He was a charter member of the U.S. Chamber of Commerce, and President Herbert Hoover tapped him to be a part of a special Depression-era commission to deal with problems pertaining to business and unemployment. Above all, though, Samuel was a blunt, energetic man, who was always active in a host of activities. Samuel's legacy to his children and grandchildren was his example of selfless giving to others, and of getting involved in civic and political activities in an attempt to make the world a better place.

Flora Sheldon Bush

Great-Grandmother
of the president

★ WHO IS FLORA BUSH ANYWAY? She's the great-grandmother of George W. Bush and mother of Prescott Bush, who was the first member of the Bush clan to venture into political office in Washington, D.C.

A s the great-grandmother of George W. Bush, Flora Sheldon Bush is the matriarch of today's newest political dynasty. While her husband was the first Bush family member to get involved in politics, her influence in the family home and in Columbus, Ohio, society, is what shaped the lives of future generations of Bushes.

Her Early Years

Flora Sheldon was born on St. Patrick's Day, March 17, 1872 in Franklin County, Ohio, to Mary Butler Sheldon and Robert Emmet Sheldon.

Little is known about her life until 1894, when she married railroad executive Samuel Prescott ("S.P.") Bush. He was an extremely influential and powerful man in the city of Columbus, Ohio, and the couple lived very well.

A Good Life

Flora and Samuel had four children together, two boys and two girls. Their oldest child, Prescott Bush, would go on to become a U.S. senator from Connecticut.

Full Name
Flora Sheldon Bush

Birth Date
March 17, 1872

Death Date
September 4, 1920

Birthplace
Franklin County, Ohio

Marital Status
Married to
Samuel Prescott Bush

Children
Two girls and two boys,
including George W.'s
grandfather, Prescott

The couple belonged to all of Columbus' prestigious social clubs and took an active part in the city's social life. Samuel and Flora enjoyed teas, lunches, dinners and balls with the other members of Columbus society.

Columbus during these years was described by one writer as having "a certain ambiance . . . a nice balance between urbanity and the solid farm philosophy that was so pervasive in the agricultural countryside" that made it a very desirable city in which to live.

Flora didn't spend all of her time in Ohio, however. Since she and her husband were fairly affluent, Flora and her children were able to spend part of their summer (while Samuel stayed behind to work) in the resort towns along the Cape Cod, Massachusetts, coastline.

Living In Marble Cliff

Flora and Samuel built a beautiful stone mansion in the Bexley neighborhood of Marble Cliff, a middle-class suburb of Columbus, Ohio. The home was renowned for its beautiful gardens and stands today .

A Tragic Death

Flora's life met a tragic end when she was hit by a car and killed in Watch Hill, Rhode Island, in 1920 at the age of 48. S.P. would go on to marry again about five years later.

Prescott
Bush

Grandfather
of the president

Bettmann/CORBIS

★ WHO IS PRESCOTT BUSH ANYWAY? A former Senator from Connecticut and a Wall Street financier, Prescott Bush was the father of the nation's 41st President, George Bush.

Prescott Sheldon Bush leaves his greatest mark on history books as the father and grandfather of the 41st and 43rd presidents of the United States. This seems like an inadequate statement about a man who was the first Bush to win an elected office, as senator from Connecticut for 10 years. He's also the first Bush Yale graduate, and he used his Yale connections to become a wealthy Wall Street investment banker. He served on the boards of many major corporations, including CBS and the Prudential Insurance Company of America – to name a few. Today, when people talk about a Bush "dynasty" in tones comparable to the Kennedys, they often forget to look to the early 20th century for its origins.

Full Name
Prescott Sheldon Bush

Birth Date
May 15, 1895

Death Date
October 8, 1972

Birthplace
Columbus, Ohio

What He's Best Known For
U.S. senator
from Connecticut

Marital Status
Married to
Dorothy Walker Bush

Children
Prescott Jr., George,
Nancy, Jonathan
and William

A Devotion To Duty

Prescott Sheldon Bush was a man who was, in the words of his son, George Bush, dedicated to "duty and service." A man of wealth, stature, education, and lineage, Prescott appears the embodiment of uncompromising family values. His grandson, George W. Bush, has aptly described this sense, saying, "My dad would talk about my grandfather's lesson – before you enter public service you go out and make some money and take care of your family. But my grandfather

George Bush Presidential Library

believed money wasn't how you measured your life. If you had money it came with an obligation to serve." Prescott lived those words and passed them onto his heirs; his influence can be seen repeatedly in their lives.

Born in Columbus, Ohio, in 1895 to Samuel Prescott Bush and Flora Sheldon Bush, Prescott learned from his parents many of the lessons and traits that would follow the Bush family into the 21st century. His father was educated, energetic

Beginning a family tradition, Prescott played on the Yale baseball team.

and athletic. A tall, handsome man, he had a commanding presence. He was a successful businessperson, the president of the Buckeye Steel Castings Company. In college, his father played baseball – perhaps from him comes the Bush affinity for the sport.

The Beginnings Of A Dynasty

Befitting his station in life, Prescott received an education at St. George's School in Newport, Rhode Island, and then went on to Yale. There he instituted a family tradition, membership in the secretive and selective Skull and Bones Society. Upon graduation, he served an unremarkable two years in World War I. After the war, his career path led him to St. Louis, where he met and later married Dorothy Walker, daughter of George Herbert Walker, a successful investment banker. From their union came five children, a girl and four boys – including George Herbert Walker Bush, who was named for his maternal grandfather.

Greenwich, Connecticut Town Representative Prescott at work at a 1946 town meeting.

Prescott and Dorothy's 51 years together found them enjoying an extremely comfortable lifestyle with homes in such affluent towns as Greenwich, Connecticut; Kennebunkport, Maine; and Hobe Sound, Florida. He offered financial security and firm discipline, while she provided strength and compassion. Their homes were ample, but not overly fancy. In their daughter Nancy's opinion, as Midwesterners, social rank was moot to them. Yes, they had money, but with the money came obligation.

Political Leanings

Prescott filled that obligation in many ways. He was the moderator of the Greenwich, Connecticut town meeting for 17 years. He served this and other political posts (while commuting daily to Wall Street) in Connecticut, before shifting his full-time efforts from business to politics. After an unsuccessful run for the Senate as a Republican in 1950, he went on to capture the Connecticut Senate seat in 1952, defeating Abraham Ribicoff.

He spent 10 years in Washington and was regarded as an Eisenhower "middle-of-the-roader." In a CBS *Face the Nation* interview, he offered the opinion that Eisenhower Republicans had taken "the best out of the traditional positions of the Democrat and Republican party, and put them together in what the president calls the moderate progressivism of our new Republican party . . . " In fact, he was an avid civil rights supporter and promoted subsidized public assistance. His liberal stance is not surprising since his father was a Democrat. It may be that as a Republican, Prescott started the conservative-leaning trend of the Bush clan.

Another President

Prescott Bush was an avid golfer and even served as president of the United States Golf Association.

Passing On The Torch

After 10 years on Capitol Hill, Prescott chose not to run for another Senate term because of his poor health, and retired in 1962. He often regretted that decision, saying, "Once you've had the exposure to politics that I had . . . it gets in your blood, and then when you get out, nothing else satisfies that in your blood." So he had to satisfy his cravings vicariously through his son, George, who picked up the political baton from his father. When George lost the Texas Senate seat in 1970 to Lloyd Bentsen, Prescott and Dorothy were there to comfort him. But in George's opinion, his dad never intruded or forced his political opinions on his son. When asked about the best piece of advice his father ever gave him, George responded, "He never did. Ever. Of any kind whatsoever. That is kind of the model [for] the way Bushes go about this."

Prescott requests adjournment during a heated debate of the Senate Stockpiling Investigating Committee in 1962.

Prescott's Politics

Prescott served in the Senate during the height of the McCarthy era and was a strong opponent of McCarthy and his methods, voting to censure him in 1954.

Prescott was known as a stern man, one who would demand that his sons wear ties and jackets to dinner. He even insisted that his children "call me Senator."

At age 77, death came quickly to Prescott. Diagnosed in September with lung cancer, he died in less than a month on October 8, 1972. His son George has said, "He had a powerful impact on the way we came to look at the world." So, if history books "short sell" Prescott and his impact on the world, so be it. His family and friends will always have their own definition of importance – a definition that he helped them to craft by his example.

Dorothy Walker Bush

Bettmann/CORBIS

Grandmother
of the president

★ WHO IS DOROTHY BUSH ANYWAY? The mother of George Bush, our 41st president, Dorothy instilled values in her children that have remained with them throughout their lives.

Dorothy Walker Bush was the daughter of George Herbert and Lucretia Wear Walker. She was bred and educated according to her class – private schools in St. Louis and then sent East to Miss Porter's School in Farmington, Connecticut for finishing.

Ruling The Roost

She supported her husband, Prescott Sheldon Bush, throughout his career as a Wall Street investment banker and later as a senator from the state of Connecticut. While job and duty kept her husband away for long hours, Dorothy, or Dotty as she was known, provided a rock-solid foundation as well as a spirited role model to their five children.

Full Name
Dorothy Walker Bush

Birth Date
July 1, 1901

Death Date
November 19, 1992

Birthplace
Kennebunkport, Maine

Marital Status
Married to
Prescott Sheldon Bush

Children
Prescott Jr., George,
Nancy, Jonathan
and William

Religion was important to Dorothy's parents, and when raising her own family, Dorothy made sure that they didn't miss Sunday services at the Episcopal Church. She also regularly "served" scriptures with the meals. Dotty was far from one-dimensional, however. She was as tough and competitive as she was genteel. "Mother was a first-rate athlete," wrote her son George. "I don't recall a footrace Mother was ever in that she didn't come in first."

AFP/CORBIS

A fine matriarch – Dorothy (second from right) poses with her husband, Prescott (right), her son George and his, wife Barbara, in 1948. Who's the little boy wearing cowboy boots? That's George W.!

Above all, however, Dorothy Walker Bush was a mother to her children. Together with her husband, she set high standards for them. Among her rules were maxims like "never brag, never quit, never let them know you are hurting, be honest, be kind, and don't look down on anyone." As her son George described, his mother taught him about "dealing with life in an old-fashioned way of bringing up a family – generous measures of both love and discipline." Even when they were adults, she would remind her brood not make themselves seem overly important. Only a mother can demand that of a politician! Her devotion to her children was fully reciprocated – while president, George called her every day.

Biker Babe

Dotty's athleticism didn't flag in her later years. When she visited George in China at age 73, she bicycled with him through the streets of Beijing. He recalls, "You should have seen the people stare at old momma on the bicycle."

George
Bush

Father
of the president

George Bush Presidential Library

★ WHO IS GEORGE BUSH ANYWAY? The 41st president of the United States of America, George Bush is also the father of current president George W. Bush.

Although George Bush has long been associated with Texas – indeed, he and wife Barbara have a home in Houston – he was actually born in Milton, Massachusetts, and raised in Greenwich, a Connecticut suburb.

New England Beginnings

George Herbert Walker Bush came into the world on June 12, 1924, the second child of Prescott and Dorothy Bush. He grew up with his three brothers and one sister in an 11-room Victorian house and attended Greenwich Country Day School.

As a child, George was nicknamed "Little Pop" because of his adulation of his maternal grandfather, George "Pop" Walker. That nickname eventually evolved to

Full Name
George Herbert
Walker Bush
Birth Date
June 12, 1924
Birthplace
Milton, Massachusetts
Resides
Houston
What's He Up To?
Enjoying retirement
Marital Status
Married to
Barbara Pierce Bush
Children
George W., Robin
(deceased), Jeb, Neil,
Marvin and Dorothy

"Poppy," a name that, as he grew older, he successfully shook. His parents were careful to instill good values in their offspring, and mornings in the Bush household often began with his mother or father reading a Bible passage at the breakfast table.

When George was 13, he was sent to Phillips Academy in Andover, Massachusetts, a prestigious prep school. There, he excelled at sports, especially soccer, basketball and baseball. A glimpse of his future in politics may have been seen in his senior year, when he was elected class president.

The War Years

During his senior year in Andover, World War II was heating up, and, like many others his age, George resolved to fight for his country. On his 18th birthday, a few days after his graduation, George enlisted. He was the Navy's youngest pilot when he earned his wings, and was assigned to the South Pacific as a bomber pilot. During World War II, George flew a total of 58 missions.

The war ended for George on September 2, 1944 when his torpedo bomber was hit by Japanese anti-aircraft fire over the South Pacific. He bailed out into the ocean and was rescued by a submarine, but his crew perished in the attack.

Joining The Ivy League

After he returned home, George married Barbara Pierce, a young woman he had met at a country club Christmas dance in Greenwich in 1941. The two had become engaged before George left for the war

Family Tree

Prescott	Flora
Father	Mother
Born 1895	Born 1901

George	Barbara
41st President	Former First Lady
Born 1924	Born 1925

George W.	Robin	Jeb	Neil	Marvin	Dorothy
Son	Daughter	Son	Son	Son	Daughter
Born 1946	1949-1953	Born 1953	Born 1955	Born 1956	Born 1959

All In The Family

George Bush, his three brothers, father, four uncles and his son, George W. Bush, have all attended Yale University.

and George and Barbara were married on January 6, 1945 in Barbara's hometown of Rye, New York.

The newlyweds soon arrived in New Haven, Connecticut, where George, on the G.I. Bill, began his studies at Yale University. George distinguished himself while at Yale in several ways. Always an excellent first baseman, he was captain of the Yale baseball team when they made the national collegiate finals. Socially, he was tapped to join the Skull and Bones society, Yale's oldest and most secret society. Academically, he succeeded as well, completing a degree in economics in less than three years and graduating Phi Beta Kappa in 1948.

George and Barbara are enjoying retirement and performing their roles as patriarch and matriarch of the Bush clan.

Go West, Young Man

After graduation, it was time for the family (which by now included son George W.) to decide on their next move. George decided to go to Texas to make his fortune in the oil fields. So George packed up his 1947 Studebaker (a graduation gift from his parents) and drove to Odessa, Texas, where the family lived briefly before settling in Midland. Here, George had his first foray into politics when he worked for Dwight Eisenhower's presidential campaign.

In Midland, George eventually opened his own independent oil exploration firm, Zapata Petroleum, in 1954. Although he prospered in oil, George's political ambition continued to burn, and in 1964, now living in Houston, he ran for the Senate, but lost.

Ups And Downs

George suffered some hardships in his personal life in those early Texas years, the most difficult being the death of his daughter Robin in 1953. Robin was only three when she died, and the loss hit George hard. In a letter written to his mother around 1958, George wrote, "We need a girl. We had one once – she'd fight and cry and play and make her way just like the rest. But there was about her a certain softness . . . Her peace made me feel strong, and so very important . . . But she is still with us. We need her and yet we have her. We can't touch her, and yet we can feel her." (Shortly after that letter was written, in 1959, Barbara gave birth to her sixth and last child, Dorothy Walker Bush.)

George Bush Presidential Library

George Bush and daughter Robin in a loving moment.

No Respect For The President

When Bush became president, a reporter asked him if people treated him differently now. He replied, "A little bit. But Barbara and the kids treat me with the same degree of irreverence that they always have. They keep me down to earth."

Political Ambitions

In 1966, George was elected to Congress, and the family moved to Washington, D.C. In 1970, President Richard Nixon appointed George as the U.S. Ambassador to the United Nations and in 1972, Nixon selected him to head the Republican National Committee. The next president, Gerald Ford, appointed George as U.S. envoy to China, and he and Barbara lived in Beijing for a year. George hoped to be selected as a vice-presidential running mate in the 1976 election, but was instead offered the post of CIA director, which he accepted.

The Road To The White House

In 1980, George decided to make his own run for the presidency. He lost the GOP party nomination to Ronald Reagan, who then tapped George to be his running mate. The Reagan-Bush ticket won, and served from 1980-1988. When Reagan was injured in an assassination attempt, George earned praise for the way he handled the crisis, particularly when he vetoed suggestions that he land his helicopter on the White House lawn to dramatize the fact that someone was still in charge.

Bush made himself at home in the White House soon after his inauguration. Here, he sits in the Oval Office on January 21, 1989.

After serving as vice president for eight years, George made another run for the presidency in 1988 and this time, he won, He and Barbara, along with their dog, Millie, moved from the vice president's home into the White House in 1989.

George's four years in the White House were marked by the end of the Cold War, the falling of the Berlin Wall and the reunification of East and West Germany. His presidency also encountered turmoil in the Persian Gulf, culminating in Operation Desert Storm.

While he was president, George continued to vacation at Kennebunkport, Maine, and made time for his kids and grandkids. One biographer has called him "the quintessential family man, one who enjoys spending time with his family above all else."

An avid sportsman, George could often be seen piloting his powerboat, *Fidelity*, on the waters of the Atlantic off Walker's Point, as the Kennebunkport home is called. He also enjoyed jogging, fishing, golf, tennis and horseshoes, and even had a horseshoe pit installed at the White House!

Back On The Ranch

In 1992, George Bush ran for re-election and was defeated by Democrat Bill Clinton. Although no longer in the White House, George has remained active. One of his more memorable projects was the establishment of the George Bush Presidential Library and Museum on the grounds of Texas A&M University in College Station, Texas. He has stayed physically active as well, proving his fitness in a 1997 skydive which received international press attention. He recently said that he plans another skydive for 2004, when he will be 80 years old.

He and Barbara have a home in Houston, which they built after leaving the White House, and the couple still spends a great deal of

George Bush Presidential Library

time in their Kennebunkport home. Soon after he left the White House, George was quoted as saying of his post-presidential life, "I make the coffee, Barbara makes the beds, and we're right back to square one, where we got married when we were 20 years old. She does the cooking and I do the dishes and life is absolutely wonderful."

The proud parents with their son, George W. and his wife, Laura, in June of 1999.

Barbara
Bush

AP/WWP

Mother
of the president

★ WHO IS BARBARA BUSH ANYWAY? The wife of former president George Bush, Barbara Bush is one of America's most popular First Ladies. Her warmth, humor and strength have endeared her to millions of Americans.

Family and friends are the basis of former First Lady Barbara Bush's life. The mother of five and grandmother of 14 has devoted her life to raising her family and making the world a better place through her tireless efforts to combat illiteracy, something she calls "the most important issue we have."

The Early Years

Born on June 8, 1925, Barbara was raised in the affluent suburb of Rye, New York. Her father, Marvin Pierce, was the publisher of the McCall's Corporation, and was a descendant of Franklin Pierce, the 14th president of the United States. Her mother Pauline was the daughter of an Ohio Supreme Court justice. From her, Barbara inherited her love of gardening and needle-

Full Name
Barbara Pierce Bush
Birth Date
June 8, 1925
Birthplace
New York City
Resides
Houston
What's She Up To?
Active in several charities, including the Barbara Bush Foundation For Family Literacy
Marital Status
Married to George Herbert Walker Bush
Children
George W., Robin (deceased), Jeb, Neil, Marvin and Dorothy

point. In her autobiography, *Barbara Bush: A Memoir,* she says, "My mother was a striking beauty who left the world a more beautiful place than she found it. She grew lovely flowers, did the finest needlepoint I have ever seen, and knew how to keep an exquisite home." As for her father, whom she adored, Barbara has said, "He spoiled me rotten." Barbara Pierce was the third of four children. Her older sister, Martha, was considered a great beauty, while her older brother Jimmy was "feisty." Her younger brother Scott had medical problems (from which he eventually recovered), and was often in and out of the hospital.

George Bush Presidential Library

Barbara and George walk their dog.

In her sophomore year of high school, Barbara was sent to Ashley Hall, a boarding school in South Carolina. She and her friends often attended dances while home from school on holiday breaks, and it was at one such dance that she met the man who would become her husband, partner and, as she has put it, her "hero."

Barbara, The C.O.O.

Of his life growing up, Jeb Bush was quoted as saying, "Dad was the chief executive officer, but Mother was the chief operating officer. We all reported to her. She did a good job of keeping the family intact."

The year was 1941, and it was a Christmas dance in Connecticut. Sixteen-year-old Barbara was asked to dance by a handsome young man named Poppy Bush (George's childhood nickname was "Poppy"). He was 17, and a senior at Phillips Academy in Andover, Massachusetts. The two fell in love and became engaged a year and a half later.

George went off to World War II as a Navy fighter pilot, and Barbara attended Smith College in Northampton, Massachusetts (from which she later withdrew to marry George). The two were wed on January 6, 1945 and the couple honeymooned at the Cloisters resort on Sea Island, Georgia.

Story Time

In 1990, Barbara Bush hosted a weekly radio program called "Mrs. Bush's Story Time," in which she read aloud from her favorite children's books.

Sadness Strikes

The newlyweds moved to New Haven, Connecticut, where George attended Yale. He graduated in 1948 and the family, which now included two-year-old George W., moved to Odessa, Texas. George hoped to make a fortune in the oil business. He prospered, but the young family was soon struck by tragedy when their second child, Robin, was diagnosed with leukemia. She passed away in 1953, just shy of her fourth birthday.

Barbara and daughter Robin, who died of leukemia in 1953, in a light moment.

Barbara has said of that difficult time, "I nearly fell apart. I couldn't put my right foot in front of my left, but George didn't let me retreat." She pulled out of it when she realized that she was hurting her family.

Although Robin's death was tragic for Barbara, she says that her death has made her a more compassionate person. She has said, "Because of Robin, George and I love every living human more."

Time To Move

In 1959, the Bushes moved to Houston. Then, in 1966, George was elected to Congress and the Bush family moved once again, this time to Washington, D.C. By this time, Barbara and George had five

A Nervous Mother

During George W.'s presidential election campaign, Barbara couldn't stand to listen radio or television news reports on his progress. She didn't like to hear if the media felt he was doing poorly, and she didn't want to hear anything negative about her beloved son. George W.'s father, though, wanted to listen to the news reports, so Barbara asked him to use headphones, so she wouldn't have to hear any of it.

active children – George, Jeb, Neil, Marvin and Dorothy – and Barbara found herself spending all her time as "Cub Scout mother, car-pool driver and Sunday school teacher."

When George was appointed ambassador to the United Nations in 1971, it was time to move again, this time to New York City. Two years later, it was back to D.C. as chairman of the Republican National Committee, and then, in 1974, Barbara and George spent a year in Beijing when George was named U.S. envoy to China. But a year later, it was time to return to the United States, when President Ford selected George to head the Central Intelligence Agency.

Upon returning to the United States, Barbara fell into depression. Her children had all left home, and because of the nature of George's work with the CIA, he couldn't talk about it with her. She says that her feelings of emptiness and depression were exacerbated by menopause and the beginnings of the women's movement, which questioned the ideals of motherhood and family to which she had devoted her life. She eventually overcame her depression, however, and now says, "I'm glad I went through it. Now when people say they are depressed, I know."

It's A Dog's Life

In 1980, George Bush was selected as Ronald Reagan's running mate and became the vice president of the United States. Barbara devoted herself to literacy efforts during these years her husband was vice president. She

On The Road

By the time George Bush became President, Barbara Bush had moved her family 29 times due to her husband's career.

"Bar" Bush

Barbara Bush is often referred to as "Bar" by her husband. That name isn't a diminutive form of Barbara – it has a more unusual source! During the war, gas and tires were rationed, so the Bushes used a wagon pulled by a horse named Barsil, which George's brother used to teasingly call her. The name was shortened to "Bar" and stuck.

wrote a book about the family cocker spaniel called *C. Fred's Story.* She donated the proceeds to two literacy groups, Laubach Literacy Action and Literacy Volunteers of America. In 1990, while her husband was president, Barbara wrote another book, this time about a different dog – Millie, the Bushes' springer spaniel. The book was called *Millie's Book,* and it was supposedly written by Millie (as dictated to Barbara). *Millie's Book* became a bestseller, and all of the proceeds, (totalling almost $1 million), went to fund literacy programs, Barbara's favorite cause.

1600 Pennsylvania Avenue

In 1988, George Bush became the 41st president of the United States. As first lady, Barbara was occasionally asked for her opinions on political issues, or to comment on decisions that her husband had made. Barbara was always sure to make it clear that she did not care to speak about politics in public.

George Bush Presidential Library

As their helicopter lands, members of the "first family" scramble to catch up with Millie and one of her brood in 1992.

Back To Reality

George served one term as president, and in 1993, it

was back to Houston. There were some adjustments to make, such as driving a car for the first time in 12 years, but Barbara is enjoying the

George Bush Presidential Library

The former first lady shares the joys of reading with some of her many grandchildren in this 1988 photo.

post-White House years. When the Bushes are at their home in Houston, she rises at 5:00 a.m., walks their dog, Sadie, then gets back in bed to have coffee and read the paper. Her days are spent writing in her diary, working on her scrapbooks, having lunch with friends, and, of course, continuing her charity work. She says, "We're having fun. Life continues to be an adventure."

The Bush family still gathers at Walker's Point, their Kennebunkport, Maine, summer home. Barbara was recently quoted as saying, "Last summer we brought home 12 grandkids after the convention. They go to the beach. They boat, play tennis and swim for hours."

With the election of her son, George W., Barbara becomes the only first lady ever to see her son become president. When that fact was pointed out to her, she said, "Do you know how much I care about that? Zero. I don't feel like a first lady at all. I feel like a mother and a friend." Down-to-earth words from a down-to-earth woman.

Telling Her Own Story

In 1994, Barbara wrote another book, this time without the help of her canine friends. It was called *Barbara Bush: A Memoir* and chronicled her fascinating life by giving readers a peek into her diaries, which she has meticulously kept over the years.

Roots Of The Family Tree

The Bush family tree is deeply rooted in this country's early history, and can even be traced back to the throne of England. Let's meet some of the early pioneers of the "Bush dynasty."

Back To Their Roots

James Smith Bush, George W. Bush's great-great-grandfather, was an Episcopalian minister and a distant cousin to English royalty. He lived in New York with his wife, **Harriet Eleanor Fay.**

George W. Bush's great-grandfather, **George Herbert Walker** (named after the religious poet, George Herbert) was an investment banker. He opened his own firm but is best known as the founder of golf's Walker Cup. George also built the home on Walker's Point in Kennebunkport, Maine, that the entire Bush clan uses to this day as a vacation spot.

A Welcome Addition

The marriage of **Barbara Pierce** to **George Bush** added more political, business and societal lineage into the mix. The name "Pierce" was well-known in the publishing industry – Barbara's father, **Marvin Pierce,** had become president and chairman of the board of the McCall's Corporation, the publishing company that produced both *Redbook* and *McCall's* magazines.

CORBIS

Not only did Barbara come from high society, but she is also a distant relative of **Franklin Pierce.** Pierce was the 14th president of the United States. During his administration, Pierce faced issues concerning the building of the railroad and political turmoil that was a precursor to the Civil War.

Franklin Pierce (1804-1869) was the 14th president of the United States of America.

Recent History

Within the past few years, there hasn't been much talk about George Bush's siblings. George W. Bush has three uncles and one aunt – Prescott Jr., Nancy, Jonathan and William ("Bucky") – on his father's side of the family

Prescott Jr. made a name for himself in 1982 when he ran unsuccessfully for the U.S. Senate representing Connecticut – a position his father, Prescott Sr., had held previously.

Nancy, the only daughter of Dorothy and Prescott, is known as the most liberal of the clan and is an active supporter of the environment and civil rights.

Jonathan and **Bucky** stayed away from the political scene and took on the world of finance like their grandfather, George Herbert Walker.

Senator Kit Bond (left) of Missouri shakes the hand of Bucky Bush after addressing a victory celebration for his nephew, George W., on March 7, 2000.

Operating in different parts of the country, both brothers are successful businessmen who have supported two generations of Bush presidential campaigns.

Bucky lives in St. Louis, Missouri. and is the co-founder and chairman of the investment firm Bush-O'Donnell & Co. Jonathan Bush founded J. Bush & Co. in New Haven, Connecticut – not far from Yale University, the school many of Jonathan's family members have attended. He is also the president and chief executive officer of Riggs Investment Management Corporation.

Many influences have shaped the generations of the Bush family. As a family that is very connected to its roots, it is likely that future generations will continue to follow the roads that their ancestors have traveled before them, and that the youngest Bushes will achieve much the same degree success as their predecessors.

On The Campaign Trail

Uncertain of whether or not he wanted to run, George W. met often in 1998 with political heavyweights who had been involved as advisers to other great Republican leaders. With his quick wit, self-deprecating humor and friendly demeanor, George W.'s advisers were convinced that he was the man to win back the White House for the Republicans.

George W. often became animated and used his quick wit and sense of humor to invigorate crowds.

The Big Three

George W. was the main Republican party candidate throughout most of the election process. Nonetheless, there were a few familiar, and not-so-familiar, faces that threatened to steal the spotlight.

Elizabeth Dole, wife of former Republican party nominee Bob Dole and a political hopeful in her own right, made advances that looked like warm-ups for a presidential campaign. Due to a lack of funds, however, she dropped out of the race in October of 1999 and announced her support for then-Governor George W. Bush the week of the New Hampshire primary.

Gimme a "W"! Supporters hoist this welcome sign at Austin-Bergstrom International Airport in Austin, Texas just before Election Day.

U.S. Senator John McCain from Arizona also campaigned for the Republican nomination and won the all-important New Hampshire primary. Before the primary, he could be seen traveling around in his tour bus called the Straight Talk Express. When he lost the party nomination, he graciously gave his support for George W. and later they even made some campaign stops together in Florida.

George Gets His Due

At the Republican National Convention in Philadelphia, the party showed its support for George W. with speakers like Elizabeth Dole, John McCain and George's wife Laura rallying to his cause. Finally, on August 3, 2000, George W. made his

John McCain greets Bush supporters in Portland, Oregon.

own speech to accept the nomination of his party. He expressed his intention of being a president who would lead the country with action, not just words. He pledged an end to the current era of "Clintonism," and accused the government of resting on its laurels. It was also his

goal to restore honor and integrity to the presidency. George W. then outlined the main points of his platform which included reform to the educational system, social security and Medicare, as well as tax cuts and a bulking up of the military.

George W. addresses the convention as his father, mother and daughter Jenna look on.

Time To Kiss Those Babies!

Now that Al Gore had been nominated as the Democratic presidential hopeful, the campaign was on in earnest. The time of speeches, meet-and-greets and press conferences had begun. Gore and George W. focused their efforts largely in the so-called "battleground states" of Florida, Michigan, Pennsylvania and Gore's home state of Tennessee, where the winning margin between the candidates was extremely small.

Both candidates made television appearances on popular shows like *The Oprah Winfrey Show*, *The Tonight Show With Jay Leno* and *Late Night With David Letterman*. There were also three televised presidential debates in October of 2000 during which the candidates faced off on the issues confronting the United States.

George W. caught up with the late night crowd when he dropped by the set of *The Late Show With David Letterman* in October of 2000.

By this point, George W. had already put together a little more than $30 million in campaign funds to use in his battle against Gore and his supporters. Much of this monetary success was due to George W.'s "Pioneers," who vowed to each raise $100,000 in denominations of $1,000 in checks. None of George W.'s opponents (either before or after the candidates were nominated by their respective parties) ever came close to challenging the amount that he had raised.

Off The Beaten Track

In an effort to register (and win over) the almost countless number of Generation X voters, many groups sought this population out in an effort to encourage political awareness and educate them on the issues surrounding the 2000 election. Among those to latch on to the cause were the youth-centered broadcast company, MTV.

On September 26, 2000, Al Gore greeted young voters for MTV's *Choose Or Lose 2000*.

They devised a "Choose Or Lose" program, which brought campaign issues directly into the young peoples' living rooms.

The World Wrestling Federation (WWF) also got into the campaign hoopla, and introduced a "Smackdown Your Vote!" initiative. The WWF also hoped to get the presidential candidates some exposure in their wrestling venues: they asked George W. and Gore to appear at a wrestling event and even went so far as to suggest an arm-wrestling match between the pair. These ideas, however, never became a reality.

Meet The Press

George W. and his bus-full of advisors were able to capably handle every challenge to his character and history that arose. George W. was attacked early on in the campaign in regard to allegations of drug use during his college days. Reporters hounded him for information and newspapers printed scandalous headlines, but George W. refused to comment on these issues and distanced himself from the press. Surprisingly, this tactic worked, as eventually the public moved on to other

Stop the presses! As the vote narrowed, Pennsylvania's *The Express-Times* changed their story.

political issues and forgot all about the drug-use allegations. This lull turned out to be, however, just the calm before the storm.

Just days before Election Day, reports surfaced that George W. had a decades-old drunk driving charge against him. This allegation had never come up before, despite George W.'s other political campaigns. He quickly pulled himself up by his cowboy bootstraps to face the press and the public, and acknowledged that the charge was indeed true. He assured the American public that he was, after all, merely a human and had changed his ways in the many subsequent years. But, after all the scandalous happenings in the Oval Office in the past few years, would a verbal assurance be enough for the American public to turn the other cheek? No one was quite sure how this new information would affect voters.

A rally was held outside Florida's capital building in December 0f 2000.

Election Day At Last

One has to wonder what was going through George W.'s mind as he prepared for the festivities of November 7, 2000 – Election Day. Certainly, he figured that within 24 hours, he'd either be on his way to the White House or heading back to the governor's mansion in Texas. Unfortunately, it didn't turn out to be quite that simple.

A long, drawn-out election controversy would ensue, leaving the country hanging for 36 very long days. But in the end, George W. Bush would prevail, and become the nation's 43rd president.

The Historic Election Of 2000

What should have been standard government practice turned into a media circus as people everywhere wondered, who won the presidency? Confusion reigned and accusations flew for 36 days following the election, from November 7th to December 12th. Now that the smoke has finally cleared, and a winner has been declared, here's a look at the events that sparked this national controversy.

Down To The Wire

After campaigning long and hard, both candidates could only sit back and wait for the American public to cast their votes. When the polls opened on November 7th, no one was certain who would emerge the victor, since public opinion was almost evenly split. As the evening wore on, states began to report their results to the media. The torch was passed from one candidate to the other as a neck-and-neck race ensued.

George W. was prematurely identified as the new president on November 8th, 2000.

George W. swept most of the South and delivered a devastating blow to the Gore camp by taking Gore's home state of Tennessee. Gore, however, was doing extremely well, winning several large, important states, including California and New York.

Finally it boiled down to the state of Florida. Initial results predicted that Gore had the lead, then the lead went to George W. Newscasters everywhere announced that George W. was our next president and Gore even called George W. to congratulate him on his victory.

Stop The Presses!

However, the media soon became uncomfortable with the early declaration, as the gap between the candidates in Florida began to close. Their announcements suddenly seemed premature and Gore was put back in the race. Gore quickly called George W. to retract his concession. As coverage extend-

They all say the same thing, don't they?
As of November 9th, the race was still too close to call.

ed into the wee hours of morning, it became apparent that there would be no official results any time soon. So the media called it a night, saying only that the election was "too close to call." Both camps waited with their fingers crossed as ballot counting continued.

Oops!

The media has taken a blow to its credibility since networks prematurely announced election results. Due to several polling errors, announcers jumped the gun. Newscaster Tom Brokaw was quoted as saying, "We don't just have egg on our face – we have an omelet."

Gentlemen, Start Your Recounts

When the Election Day results from Florida were finally tallied, they named George W. the winner by a narrow margin. It was such a small number – less than 2,000 votes – that a mandatory machine recount was started. However, Gore was convinced that manual recounts were necessary in four of Florida's Democratic counties – Broward, Miami-Dade, Palm Beach and Volusia – after his staffers noticed voting irregularities there.

It's Bush By A Nose!

What Gore noticed was that candidate Pat Buchanan received a much larger percentage of votes in these counties than anywhere else in Florida and it is believed by many, and even admitted by Buchanan himself, that many of these votes were most likely intended for Gore.

Craig Waters announces the 7-0 ruling concerning the counting of tallied votes on November 21, 2000.

Most disputed votes were cast on "butterfly" ballots. The layout of these butterfly ballots caused mass confusion, since voters were unsure of how to cast their ballots on them. The ballots might have been only indented ("dimpled" or "pregnant" chads) or not punched all the way through ("hanging" chads). These ballots were considered "undervotes." There were also "overvotes" on some of the ballots, on which more than one choice for president was indicated (in most cases, both Gore and Buchanan's names were punched). Many believe that these "mis-votes" had an impact on the eventual election result.

Gentlemen, Start Your Recounts, Part II

George W was not as convinced. On November 11th, he filed a lawsuit in Miami to stop the manual recounts, but his request was denied. However, he was not deterred and George W. took his case to the appeals court.

In the meantime, the Florida Supreme Court entered the fray on November 17th. The Supreme Court prohibited Florida's Secretary of State, Katherine Harris, from certifying the election – originally planned for November 18th – so they could review the issue.

Andrew Colesanti spent his Thanksgiving holding a sign outside the counting center in West Palm Beach.

On November 21st, the Supreme Court decided to continue the recounts and set a deadline of November 26th. This didn't give the counties much time to go through the ballots again. While this was happening, George W. continued to pursue his case and the U.S. Supreme Court agreed to hear his appeal.

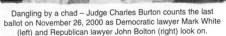

Dangling by a chad – Judge Charles Burton counts the last ballot on November 26, 2000 as Democratic lawyer Mark White (left) and Republican lawyer John Bolton (right) look on.

It's Bush By A Nose! Part II

On November 26th, Gore suffered a huge blow when Katherine Harris certified the Florida vote. Only two of the four counties had managed to complete their recount by the deadline and Harris refused to accept late results. As a result, George W. was declared the winner with a lead of 537 votes.

Gore's Last Stand

But it wasn't over yet – the courts were still battling it out. Gore made a request to the circuit court that several thousand disputed votes in Miami-Dade and Palm Beach Counties be manually recounted.

On December 1st, the U.S. Supreme Court began hearing George W.'s appeal, but sent the appeal back to the Florida Supreme Court for further clarification. Around the same time, Gore received a verdict from the circuit court denying a recount, but Gore quickly appealed to the Florida Supreme Court.

Comic Relief

Comedians had a field day with the 2000 election and its ensuing controversy. Late night hosts, humor columnists and shows like *Saturday Night Live* all parodied the political mess. Even MSNBC joined in with a special showcasing comedians' takes on the 2000 election.

Fate smiled upon Gore once again on December 8th. The Florida Supreme Court called for a manual recount of undervotes in all counties that had not already counted them.

A Supreme Effort

However, the very next day, the U.S. Supreme Court stopped all recounts and agreed to hear George W.'s appeal. Finally, late on December 12th, the U.S. Supreme Court gave its final ruling – manual recounts would not be permitted. There was no way the recounts could be completed in the few hours that remained until the deadline to select the Florida electors.

After the U.S. Supreme Court ruling, Gore had little choice. On December 13th, Gore officially conceded the election to George W. An amazing 36 days after it had begun, the election was finally over! The final bricks fell into place on December 18th, when the states' electors cast their votes, securing George W.'s position as president. Then, on January 6th, when Congress approved the electoral votes. Relief was felt everywhere – we had finally elected a new president – but a sense of bewilderment, and in some cases anger and frustration, still remained.

Not even Superman could save this election. Scott LoBaido, posing as the superhero, protests in front of the Supreme Court.

Popularity Contest

One of the intriguing subplots of the 2000 election is that Gore won the national popular vote, although George W. became the president through electoral votes. The Electoral College is the complicated, mind-boggling process of selecting a president, that boils down to: if a candidate loses a state's popular vote, even if it's by a very

History Repeats Itself

In 1876, presidential candidate Samuel J. Tilden won the popular vote over Rutherford B. Hayes. However, the votes of three states, including Florida, were disputed by the Republicans and the case went to an Electoral Commission who awarded the 20 electoral votes to Hayes, giving him the presidency.

narrow margin, they lose all of the electoral votes for that state. Therefore, states with more electors have more pull in the election than states with less electors. That's why the ballots in the state of Florida were so important.

The Aftermath

Other, more personal accusations, have been made about the election. Both sides have complained about partisanship by several of the key players. Many were wary of the fact that Jeb Bush, George W.'s brother, was Florida's governor and Harris, who would certify the election, was part of George W.'s Florida campaign. Several people also questioned the motives of the courts in making their decisions.

Allegations are being investigated by the U.S. Commission on Civil Rights regarding the Florida election. Black leaders complained that many black voters were denied access to the polls in certain areas of the state. Governor Jeb Bush has already been subpoenaed to testify. After the election, *The Miami Herald* even alleged that over one hundred votes in Florida's Miami-Dade county were cast by people who were not legally registered to vote.

Disagreeing protesters in front of the Supreme Court in Washington, D.C., December, 2000.

To further muddy the waters, several news organizations have joined together to complete a recount of the disputed votes in Florida.

Both undervotes and overvotes will be examined by an independent research firm. If their results show that Gore should have won Florida, there's no telling how it will affect George W.'s presidency.

Many look toward election reform and continued investigations to prevent this situation from reoccurring. Governor Jeb Bush has formed a panel to investigate possible reforms to the Florida election

laws and people all over the United States are suggesting reforms, such as uniform poll closing times, an electoral vote that more clearly reflects the popular vote and digital polling machines.

On December 19, 2000, in their first meeting since the debates, Bush and Gore shake hands after the Court's final ruling.

Bush has emerged as the victor of one of the closest presidential races in the United States. This historic election has sparked debate all over the country and will leave its mark on the United States for years to come. Now the American public can only wait to see what he does with his first 100 days in office, as well as the rest of his term. What will the White House be like for the next four years?

What To Expect In The Next Four Years

Many have speculated about what the White House will look like for the next four years, and what we can expect from President George W. Bush and his family. The new "first Family" will surely be compared not only to the Clintons, but to the prior Bush administration governed by George W.'s father.

Black Tie And . . . Boots?

Before they even had begun to set trends within this country's political makeup, the Bushes celebrated their victory through an impressive gala affair during Inaugural Weekend. Eight inaugural balls took place in January, 2001, but the hottest ticket in town was for the Texas State Society's Black Tie & Boots Ball. The popularity of this event may signal a coming era of parties filled with Tex-Mex food, country music and chic Washington attire mixed with western boots, not unlike the footwear that carried George W. down the campaign trail and into the White House.

Fashion is always an issue for any new administration. Remember the many fingers pointed at Hillary Rodham Clinton's

AP/WWP

Bush is perfectly comfortable in his western boots and hat and rarely goes anywhere without them.

choice of attire when she was a fledgling first lady? The fingers may have been withdrawn (or maybe were just re-directed) but they're back now and Laura Bush is the target. Laura's suits have been criticized by the media for being classic, but bland.

Both Laura and George W. will be making statements with their attire, and their fashion sense is sure to evolve over the next four years. But what can the American public expect to see? Laura Bush's longtime fashion designer, Michael

Faircloth, has the answer: "I think people will see a more tame and sophisticated side of Texas through President and Mrs. Bush," says.

The Invisible Twins

The media respectfully adhered to the Clintons' requests to keep their daughter, Chelsea, out of the limelight. Chelsea, who was not even in high school when her father was elected, is now in college and has successfully kept her private life private. It seems that Barbara and Jenna Bush will take the same route and, to date, have remained behind the scenes. The "first daughters" will most likely dodge the spotlight for the next four years, as well, which shouldn't be too difficult from behind the walls of two of this country's great institutions, Yale University and the University of Texas.

Laura, Barbara And Literacy

First ladies have a reputation for picking up charitable causes and giving them a voice for the duration of their stay in the White House. Rosalynn Carter fought for mental health awareness and Nancy Reagan is still synonymous with the "Just Say No!" drug education campaign. Barbara Bush took up the fight for literacy awareness by founding the Foundation For Family Literacy and her daughter-in-law, and current first lady, Laura Bush has fol-

As a former librarian, it's no surprise that Laura Bush champions literacy causes. Here, she reads to a second grade class in Orlando, Florida.

lowed her lead by beginning a reading initiative that brings literacy awareness to schools. She also established the Texas Book Festival, an annual celebration of writers and reading. Prepare for Laura, a former librarian and teacher, to head up more campaigns for her cause, perhaps in conjunction with her famous mother-in-law.

The White House Zoo

Presidential pets are nothing new to the White House. Cats, dogs, raccoons and even a bear have all enjoyed a romp around the presidential grounds in past administrations. Joining George W., Laura, Barbara and Jenna in the White House will be three of their "furrier" family members: Spot Fletcher, the family's English springer spaniel; Barney, a Scottish Terrier puppy given to the Bush family by Governor of New Jersey, Christine Todd Whitman; and India, a family cat sometimes referred to as Willie. Seems the White House is losing one Willie and gaining another.

The Bushes do have another cat, Ernie. A six-toed cat that was named after other six-toed cat owner Ernest Hemingway, Ernie was taken in by the Bushes after Spot chased him up a tree. Due to Ernie's destructive behavior, however, he will not be joining the family at 1600 Pennsylvania Avenue.

Can we expect more stories "told by" any of the Bush family canines? After all, Spot is a direct descendant of Millie, who penned, or maybe pawed, the best-selling, inside-the-White-House exposé that raised staggering amounts of money for former first lady Barbara Bush's personal crusade of literacy.

Presidential Menu

Ronald Reagan munched on jelly beans. George Bush hated broccoli. Bill Clinton jogged to McDonald's. For each administration, there's a food image often evoked. But what of George W? How does he feel about broccoli? More importantly, how does he feel about enchiladas? Sources say he loves them and several other types of Tex-Mex food. White House guests now know just what to expect when visiting for dinner!

George W. enjoys a hot dog during the Texas Rangers' opening day game against the White Sox in 1998.

White House Contact Information

Planning a trip to Washington, D.C.? Looking for a way to contact the First Family? There are several avenues you can take (including Pennsylvania) to find out about news, events and White House happenings.

The White House
1600 Pennsylvania Avenue NW
Washington, D.C. 20500
202-456-1414 (voice) • 202-456-2461 (fax)

Touring The White House

If you're in the area and would like to take a tour of the esteemed estate at 1600 Pennsylvania Avenue, you have two options. The White House is open for tours five days a week, Tuesday through Saturday, and you have the option of either taking the Congressional guided tour or conducting your own self-guided tour. If you are interested in the Congressional tour, be sure to plan ahead; it will take at least eight to ten weeks to secure tickets. For more information on touring the White House, call the Visitors Office at 202-456-7041. And, before you start your tour, be sure to visit the White House Visitors Center, which is chock full of video exhibits and White House memorabilia.

www.whitehouse.gov

Dedicated to all things presidential, **www.whitehouse.gov** contains information on the current president, as well as overviews of past presidents. You can take a virtual tour of the grounds, listen to recent radio addresses and find out how to contact different areas of the government. There's even a special area of the site devoted to kids! And if you'd like to contact either the president or first lady online, you can fill out one of the site's easy-to-use forms.

Photo Index

U se this index to find photographs of Bush family members, as well as other notable people whose photos appear in this book. Pages are listed in numerical order.

The Hottest Topics In America Today!

WHO ARE THESE PEOPLE Anyway?

$7.95

TV Actors & Actresses

WHO ARE THESE PEOPLE Anyway?

Hot Stars From Your Favorite Shows, Including:
- ER
- Friends
- Will & Grace
- The Practice
- Dawson's Creek
- The Sopranos
- And More!

Martin Sheen
The West Wing

Debra Messing
Will & Grace

Ray Romano
Everybody Loves Raymond

Sarah Michelle Gellar
Buffy the Vampire Slayer

Brook a Allie
Dawson's Creek

Get The Scoop On YOUR Favorite Celebrities!

Loaded With Fun Facts About Your Favorite People!

Makes A Great Gift!

Check Out Our Other Exciting Titles!

Movie Actors & Actresses
TV Newscasters
TV Talk Show Hosts
Radio Talk Show Hosts
Sports Superstars
Women In Sports
Influential Women
Pop Music Superstars
Backstreet Boys
★ NSYNC

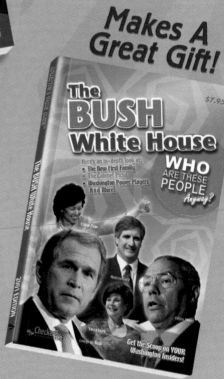

COLLECTOR'S VALUE GUIDE

The BUSH White House

$7.95

WHO ARE THESE PEOPLE Anyway?

Here's an in-depth look at:
- The New First Family
- The Cabinet Picks
- Washington Power Players
- And More!

Elaine Chao

2001 EDITION

The BUSH White House

Laura Bush

George W. Bush

Colin Powell

Get the Scoop on YOUR Washington Insiders!

Every book is in full color and features as many as 25 close-ups of people in our daily lives.

CheckerBee Publishing · 800-746-3686 · www.CheckerBee.com